Some Memories and Musings

Marilyn Lavender Cook

Copyright © 2017 by Marilyn Cook

All Rights Reserved. No part of this book may be reproduced, stored or transmitted, in any form without the prior written permission of the author.

Printed in Jacksonville, FL, USA.

ISBN 13: 978-1-61063-096-2

Library of Congress Control Number: 2017903765

Printed by OnLineBinding.com

OnLineBinding.com

1817 Florida Ave
Jacksonville, FL 32206
Phone: 904.674.0621
Fax: 904.356.3373
Email: info@onlinebinding.com

Table of Contents

Growing Up Years and Alaska
1939-1962

Marriage and Life on the Hill
1962-1986

Life in the Sunshine State
1986-1997

YWAM Harpenden/England, and Germany/Austria
1997-2002

Carribbean, Ridgecrest, La Sabranenque, New England
2003-2006

Virginia, retirement, Israel
2007-2008

China and Hawaii
2008-2009

Turkey
2009

Turkey and Switzerland
2010-2012

Turkey
2012-2013

Norway, Prague, Italy and Ireland
75th Birthday
2014-2015

Ukraine and Poland
2016

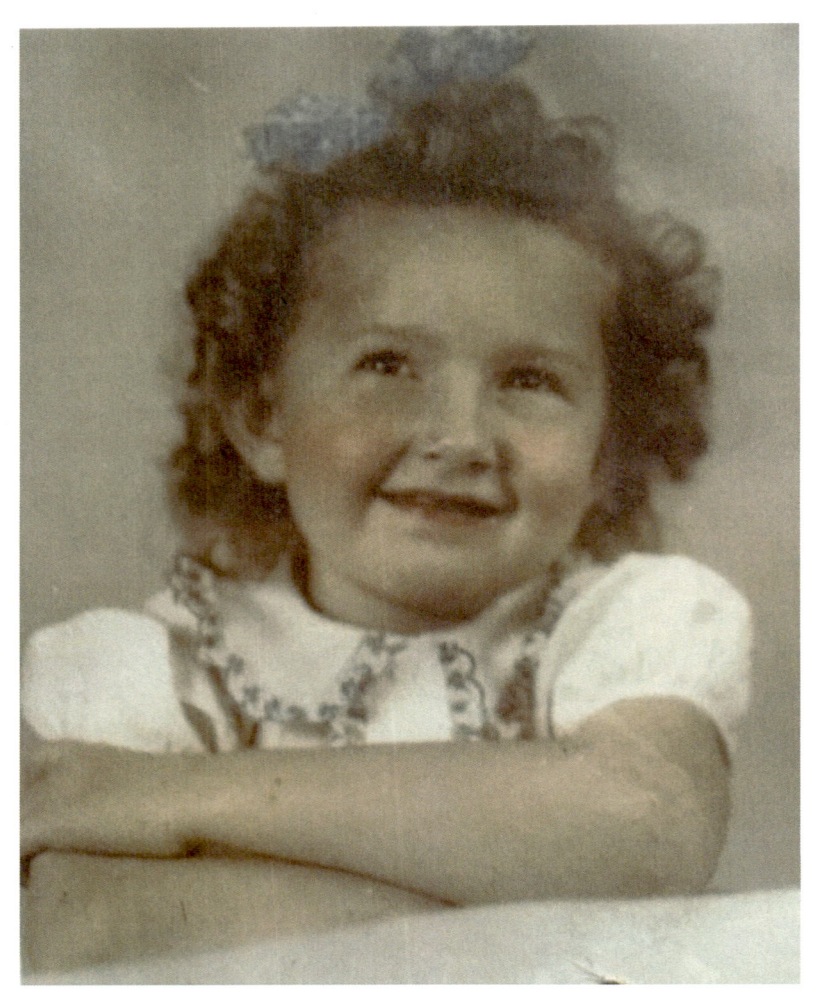

Growing Up Years
and
Alaska

1939-1962

Everybody has a story that wants telling, maybe even begs to be told. My story begins in 1939, the beginning of WWII, when the Gestapo marched on Poland. This has always registered with me and is, of late, especially interesting to me since I was in Krakow and Warsaw, and in Kiev, just this past summer, adding to my knowledge of the war in that area, even the Yalta conference that gave Stalin the spoils he wanted, the Eastern bloc countries. Poland supposedly won the war, but Poland wasn't free; those countries went from Nazi rule to Communism. It weighs on me.

I was born in Charleston, Mississippi, a small town in the hills that run alongside the Mississippi Delta. Some like to point out that Charleston was once home to the world's largest lumber mill, Lamb Fish Lumber Company. At the turn of the 20th Century, the town was one of the largest, most progressive cities in North Mississippi.

As a child we were shown where the mill was and where the large hotel was, but the town was just a typical Southern town in my childhood. We kind of lived a quiet life. The war was over. My daddy and two uncles came home and settled in.

My parents were Morris and Frances Fielder Lavender. My brothers, Jim and David. One set of grandparents to the left of us, the other set to the right. My daddy, his daddy, and my mother's daddy were carpenters. My mother was a receptionist, later a florist.

Our demographics were white citizens with the black community separate. Churches were Protestant. No ethnic diversity. Everyone's ancestors were English for the most part. In time the Catholic Church was added but thought strange at first. Desegregation of the schools became an unwanted reality for sure in 1970. Folks were Democratic. There never has been any industry to speak of since the Lamb Fish Lumber Mill. Population was @ 2,100 in the early '40's. I think it is around 2,200 now.

Charleston is a county seat. You drive down the only main street, pass the Baptist Church, the Methodist Church, keep to your right, and half circle around the court house and keep going down Main Street. When I was growing up there, the black businesses were down at the end of that street. The black community's residential area was called Smokey. Ellen lived in Smokey. She would come sometimes and help my mother and grandmother with cooking and chores. I remember Ellen sat by me and showed me the scripture that teaches children should be obedient to their parents. Ellen was like family.

I am seventy-eight years old and live in a huge sprawling metropolis in Florida. Jacksonville is on the St Johns River and on the Atlantic Ocean, becoming more multi-cultural all the time, densely populated, traffic congestion, many religious faiths, kind of a south Georgia mix with residents from the Northern states, restaurants, symphony, counter cultures, beach combers, you name it. The city is proud of our NFL team, the Jaguars. Jacksonville hosted the Super Bowl in 2005. The Patriots defeated the Eagles 24-21.

I still prefer the oak trees to the palm; deep-fried catfish and hush puppies to the shrimp.

I will always be Southern. When I was teaching in summer camp in Ireland in 2015, we had a group from Italy. The kids would say their favorite foods were pizza and pasta. Sure, no problem, but the truth is they will never know what a " boiled pot" of beans or peas is, cooked with fatback, or I think Marjorie Kinnan Rawlings called it white bacon, when she found her true self at Cross Creek, just south of here, growing things from the earth. Of course the "boiled pot" comes with crunchy cornbread, maybe potato salad with fresh green onions, a plate of sliced red tomatoes, and you can go on: fried okra, boiled cabbage, stewed squash, mustard greens, baked sweet potatoes, meat loaf, fried green tomatoes, fried chicken, biscuits and gravy, blackberry cobbler, sweet tea. God help anybody that wasn't born Southern.

I think back on all the things I have been able to experience. College, dorm life with roommates, marriage, children, being a preacher's wife, teaching, grandchildren, traveling to nearly every country in Europe. That little girl in that small town would never in a million years have thought she would see and do so much.

Where to start? I think I will go back to 1945 and pick up there. I was playing down in my grandmother's backyard, when the loudspeaker system the town used came on and said that Franklin Roosevelt had died. Roosevelt was revered in our family. My mother had worked for the WPA during the war. She needed the job and it helped so much.

My grandmother's backyard is where she washed clothes in a big black cast iron pot over a fire. She stirred them with a big pole and lifted them to a tin tub of water with blueing in it. Then to another tub with clear water. She also used those tin tubs for us to use to splash in in the summertime for fun. She would put the water in and let them sit in the sun to warm and then we would have our own swimming pool.

I remember my grandmother (we called her Marmee because she liked that the mother in <u>Little Women</u> was called Marmee) would also wring a chicken's neck in the backyard. She'd swing that chicken in the air several quick, swift circles and pop its neck.

We would make playhouses in the backyard. We laid out the floor plan with long sticks that were used for tomato plants. They were put in the ground by the plant as it grew up. Mother would tie the plant loosely with old nylon stockings to keep the shoots growing upward.

I started to school, and of course many of us went to school together all twelve years and graduated together in 1957. We had morning and afternoon recess (something the kids do not have now). We had an hour for lunch and could leave the campus. I walked the few minutes walk home and ate and went back to play softball before the bell. Junior High School stands out because Mr. and Mrs. Musslewhite taught us, as well as many generations of kids in Charleston.

I took piano lessons and would go to my grandmother's after school, have a snack and read the comics, and practice piano. My mother made doll clothes for a little girl's Santa once, to earn money for my lessons. At the end of each school year, we would have a recital in the auditorium which was on the third floor of the high school. We wore evening gowns. I was always so nervous.

My friends were: Patty Cannon, Betty Champion, Betty Bogue Ramsey, Esther Rose Jones, Sherry Williams, Lillian McNulty, Jane Smith, and Kathryn Bennett. One time I went home with Lillian because she lived in the country and I wanted to ride the school bus. That was so cool to me. I did not tell my parents. I don't know how they found me. They came to get me and they were mad.

My friends and I had big imaginations. There was no TV or electronics. We played outside. Patty and I played dress-up and movie stars a lot, wagging old clothes, cast off heels, jewelry in boxes, from her house to mine and vice versa. We also collected movie star pictures from magazines like <u>Life</u>. Betty Bogue and I dressed as pirates and went uptown playing out the drama. Lillian and I played in the country in hills and gullies cowboys and Indians. Sherry and I fashioned paper doll clothes. I still have mine. Sherry and I and Jane and Kathryn gave presentations in the 4-H Club. Betty and I modeled the dresses we made in 4-H at Mississippi State.

On Saturday afternoons, we might go to the movies and see a Western with Roy Rogers or Gene Autry. The theater was on the court square and it was 25 cents to get in. You could also go to the drug store, get a lemonade from the soda jerk, sit and read the comic books free of charge.

In the 11th grade, Willis Meek and I dated. He sat by me in Miss Allen's English class. We were breaking up when school was out. I visited him out at Cascilla. It was night. We hung on a rail fence. The moon was bright. My heart was broken. I wrote about that in an essay in college, the best grade I got all year. His wife found me on Facebook recently and sent me his picture.

Memories of Elvis. Elvis came to Charleston and played at the old gym in 1955. Proceeds at the door were $175 with @ 200 people present. He came in a pink Cadillac, a purple suit, and wore his blue suede shoes. His numbers included "That's Alright Mama" and "Danny Boy". Johnny Cash was a lead-in act. My cousin, Charles Dewey, overheard a conversation backstage of Cash berating Elvis for being late. I attended the concert. This was small potatoes. He was not yet famous in 1955.

Charleston High School   1917-1957   Charleston, MS

I was Valedictorian of our class. I wrote and gave my Valedictory address. We had the ceremony in our Baptist Church. I made my profession of faith in that church the summer before our junior year. Landrum Leavell was our pastor. I was active in YWA. I taught SS and BTU classes at the church and sang in two choirs and played the piano for a third choir for two years. Once I played "Jerusalem" for a children's choir to perform in church.

> " Jerusalem, Jerusalem, lift up your voice and sing.
> Hosanna, in the highest, hosanna to your king."

When I went to Israel in 2008, the bus was approaching Jerusalem. We could see the temple mount. They were playing that song. It was very moving. Jerusalem was the apex of our trip. One day Jesus will rule from the city of David in Jerusalem, a major crowning moment of time.

We graduated in 1957, before everything went crazy in the '60's.

> "Ike was in the White House, and Hoss was on TV.
> God was in his heaven. In the land that made me, me."

You gotta love it! During my high school years, I planned to attend Mississippi College, a private Baptist college in Clinton, MS, with a major in English and minor in Secondary Education. That freshman year- there were seven of us in our suite in Jennings Hall. Those years my closest friends were Ann Toland, Becky Grantham, and Shirley Jackson. We visited in one another's homes. I was in Ann's and Becky's wedding. We were so bonded, young and silly at times, but blessed to experience dorm life with such special people. As an English major, I was inducted into the Sigma Tau Delta, an honorary English society.

The Dean of Women met with us girls. She said, "Ladies never go out in public without a girdle." Talk about old school, but we were taught to be classy and dress and present ourselves as ladies.

I never had money in my pocket in those college years. I bought a meal ticket and my roommate and I always got up and ate breakfast in the school cafeteria, dinner, and supper. Regular as clock work. They punched the meal ticket. We hardly ever ate anywhere else. I did not go home a lot. Sometimes you could catch a ride with a ministerial student on Sundays who was preaching near my home. I might ride up with him and come back that night. Mississippi College is a private Baptist college. We were sheltered and naïve. No smoking in the girls' dorms. It is a good school. I especially remember chapel. Such good speakers and so inspirational. Our theme song was "Savior, Like a Shepherd Lead Us". My first year the cost per semester hour was $6.00. It went up to $8.00. I remember my total cost my last year was $1,000 which covered everything.

I worked in the Alumni office for 50 cents an hour. I kept the alumni addresses current and did the mailings for the college bulletin. The addresses were on cards of a thin material in a drawer. Ink is added in the machine. You put the drawer of cards in the machine and foot peddle. As the cards move across and drop, you feed the newsletter under the card for the mailing.

The first summer of my college years the Baptist Training Union took a trip to the World Youth Alliance in Toronto, Canada. The Baptist Church at home paid my way. We saw the sights in Washington, D.C., and New York City on the way up. We rocked that bus with Christian choruses on the road. The next summer I worked for the Southern Baptist Association in Leslie, Arkansas, in the Ozarks. I worked in Vacation Bible Schools. The first week I stayed in a trailer by myself, out in the dark nowhere, after that, with an elderly missionary couple. The next summer I again was with the Southern Baptists in Oklahoma working with Native Americans. I stayed with a mIssionary family in Lawton five weeks and taught in a summer camp. The other five weeks in Russellville. I stayed with a pastor and family. I remember we worked in a revival. They put a piano in the back of a pickup truck. I played for the service from that truckbed!

Joyce and I in the Ozarks

In the spring of 1961, I was a senior. I went to the library. My friend, Charlotte Parkman, was reading a letter from someone she knew who was teaching in Nome, Alaska, and trying to recruit her to come up and enjoy teaching in the land of the Arctic. She succeeded in whetting our appetites for adventure. Charlotte and I both were hooked. We arranged our applications by mail and received our contracts. I would earn $5,850 for the school year, 1961-1962, in Nome, Alaska.

So Charlotte and I took a train from Memphis to Chicago and across the majestic Rocky Mountains, past the sunset on Whitefish Lake, to Seattle. We had a friend in college who arranged for us to stay with his family enroute to our destination. I remember all of us singing hymns around the piano, a chocolate dessert to die for, the lush green profuse ferns from the constant rains in Seattle.

Time to fly to Anchorage and to Nome. The school superintendent and two friends met our plane. I wrote in my journal it was the most desolate, dreary spot I had ever seen. They took us to our house that we would rent and split the $100.00 a month rent. The house was one block down from Front Street, two blocks from the Bering Strait. We had a living room with a console radio, bedroom, nice big kitchen with a large stove for heating the house as well. I can still remember a morning when we were up early cleaning and we saw two kind of elderly women outside taking pictures. They were tourists, passing through. We, we were part of the fabric of this Arctic world. Oh, my gosh! Unbelievable for two young Southern girls embarking on the adventure of their lifetime.

I have always had fun telling about the bathroom. No plumbing for the commode, which is a wood box with a lid, that backs up to the outside wall where there is a small door that opens, so the men who come to get the buckets, can pull the used one out and put in a clean one. They are called "honey buckets".

Our house was just around the corner from our school. We were so tickled with our house we forgot the dingy, drab and monotonous look outside. The houses go on and on just the same, shacks from the outside. Streets were dirt, board sidewalks, no trees or vegetation whatever, sky pierced with poles and wires.

But the social life in Nome is so warm. People were so friendly. Right off, a neighbor brought over a loaf of bread fresh out of the oven. Just add butter and preserves. To this day I never eat raspberry preserves I don't think of a time we visited a couple in Matanuska Valley. They served homemade raspberry preserves. I am always transported back to that memory.

Charlotte and I ordered fur-lined boots from Montgomery Ward. I planned to use a pea coat that belonged to my uncle in the Coast Guard. I packed everything I took in an old trunk that also belonged to him and had that shipped separately to Nome. Charlotte had a lady make her a pretty rabbit parka.

We had a lot of fun ordering staple foods from Seattle. The order had to be in by September 8, so the ship could come in to Nome before the sea froze over. The grocery in town had fresh meat and vegetables, but everyone ordered canned goods by boat. They were cheaper that way. We were clueless but put together a list of cans of vegetables and fruits. So when the order came in, we stocked the shelves in the hallway to the back door and had our own little store.

We would get so tickled with the radio station. It is local, just for Nome. Every once in a while they would announce something personal like so-and-so wants to see so-and-so if he comes to town by a certain time. It was so funny.

School started September 6. We walked through our backyard and there was the school. We mostly walked anywhere we went except the time friends took us to Council, a ghost town from gold mining days, and the time we were invited to a camp on a weekend--- looked out the window- there was a bush plane sitting in the yard! So many memories- we went blue berry picking. The tundra is spongy. I spilled all my berries and sat down and picked them out of the mosses and lichens. The sun, shining pink upon the bottom of the mountains and yellow upon the snow-capped peaks. It's all God and there you are all alone right in the middle of it.

Another memory-the Northern Lights-dancing across the sky, changing colors and positions, green and yellow dances.

The first snow was October 1 and it stayed. Everything was beautiful after the snow. Paul Green, the janitor at school, an elderly Eskimo man, liked to visit with us and tell us stories "in early days ago" "before friend missionary came." Paul Green wrote a book, <u>I Am Eskimo</u>, <u>Aknik my Name</u>. We bought an autographed copy. Years later in a Jacksonville, Florida, book store where you can buy and sell your books, I found a copy of that book. I nearly fainted. It was autographed like mine is. This means someone else like me had known Paul Green and wound up like me in Jacksonville. Is that a strange coincidence? I had to buy that book.

Mr. Green taught us to Eskimo dance and we performed several times that year. Parkas, mukluks, gloves with yarn streamers, the works. The Eskimo men played the drums. The natives loved our performing with them.

We attended several churches and sang at times. Always there were families who had us over for a nice meal or we cooked for company. A wonderful social life. We had a fantastic Thanksgiving invite and Christmas invite. I remember walking to the Christmas dinner. It was 50 below in cold, windy Nome.

I think it is neat to explain the word "outside". If you live in the States, you are from "outside". Other words, any place outside of Alaska. And the word sourdough means a person born and bred in Alaska of course. It is also fun to share with others the dark winters and light summers as the sun would rise and set at different times. I think I remember the shortest days were from 10:00 am to 2:00 pm. The longest days, well, you could go to a movie at night and come out in broad daylight. I remember seeing a movie. The lady was leaving the house and walked outside. I caught myself wanting to yell at her, " Hey, you forgot to change to your boots. Go back and put on your boots." That was a given if you went out as well as your coat.

It was fun to walk in the snow. Ron, one of the teachers and I were walking one night. He said, "You can feel the silence tonight- sort of creeps into you." He said, "Nature plays such a big part here. Nome is only secondary and may as well not even be here. It is engulfed by something bigger than itself."

Once we did a dog team ride out in the wilderness. The dogs were tied, but straining at their leashes, jumping and cavorting and yelping. They could not wait to get on the trail. I can still see the excitement of those dogs anticipating a run. So, when we did get loaded and started out, they yanked the sled over several times and we were spilled out into the snow.

When we got out of town, there was the whiteness. Nothing to mark where the land stopped and horizon started. It was one complete vast area of whiteness. Just enveloped in white. Sky moved into land and land into sky with nothing to divide either one. Only stark white space.

The famous Iditarod race takes place in early March every year. It finishes in Nome. The first race was in 1973, so we were not a part of that in 1962. The sled dog relay that inspired the Iditarod took place in 1925. Mushers delivered life-saving serum to Nome, then a remote village suffering from a diphtheria epidemic. The Siberian husky, Balto, became famous as the lead dog on the final leg of the run. The race today is run on some of those same trails. The 1,000-mile finish culminates on Front Street.

My French classes put together a banquet. We practiced little skits in French. We raided the art supplies and painted lots of posters for an art exhibit. We did a sidewalk café and a fountain. We made an Eiffel Tower. An excellent cook helped with the cooking. This was a first for me, but it was so fun I repeated it at Strider Academy years later and at Charleston High School, both in Mississippi. And always a big success.

At the end of the year, we had a lot of canned goods left. We advertised on the radio, and a man with a large family came with a sled and bought the food stuffs!

I played in a piano recital and also for the graduation exercises at the end of the year.

I wrote several articles telling of our experiences in Alaska and they were printed in the <u>Mississippi Sun</u>. Cecil Allison saw them and wrote me a letter that he enjoyed the articles. I wrote in my journal, "I do not really know him." This is so mind-boggling to me now. I would meet him years later. He and his wife figured prominently in my life in 1986, when I had two sons in the Navy in Jacksonville, Florida. Dr. Allison was a principal in Jacksonville and offered me a job. So he was the catalyst in helping me move from Charleston, Mississippi, to teach in Florida and have a better retirement.

But, for now, my story picks up after my year in Alaska.

Marriage and Life on the Hill

1962-1986

The year was 1962. I was asked to teach at Charleston High School in my hometown. After a few paychecks I went to an orthodontist and had braces put on my teeth. I had waited years to do that. I had to settle in to a slow life style after the fast-paced year in Alaska, but it was a good school year. I remember each teacher was assigned to be in charge of an assembly. Mine was at Christmas. I had someone recap the birth of Jesus, had a Santa make his entrance with some drama, and the girls in my homeroom formed a living Christmas tree, dressed in white and holding a candle, and sang Christmas carols.

I met Jerry Cook whose family lived in the Paynes community near Charleston. We married and moved to Las Vegas, Nevada. He had two uncles and families who were in a church ministry there. I did not like the sand and no grass or trees, but we did get away and go to Hoover Dam sometimes which was really neat. And of course you have to go see the Strip. We went to see Johnny Cash perform. John Kennedy was assassinated that year on November 22, l963. I think a lot of people remember where they were when that happened. Camelot was no more. A heavy sadness hung over America.

Jerry and I moved back home after the school year. He was hired by Busch Jewelers in Vicksburg, Mississippi. We moved there and made friends at the Church of God of Prophecy pastored by Brother Overstreet. When he died and we were sitting quietly during the visitation, it was the strangest feeling. Brother Overstreet had just stepped into heaven and it felt like he and heaven were very close. Our oldest son, Chuck, was born in 1964 while we were in Vicksburg.

By 1966, Kenny was born, and Jerry was appointed to a pastorate at Spanish Fort, a small community near Yazoo City, Mississippi. We both came to life. We loved our role as pastor and pastor's wife. I was happy as a lark. We lived in a rambling house with a large fenced in yard, where perennial flowers along the fence would just pop up and surprise me, down the road aways from the church. The boys played in the screened-in porch.

Some of the crazies I remember- The house was near a pond with some fallen logs. Boocoodles of turtles would line up on those logs. If you went outside and made extra noise, they all plopped in the water.

Big rats got into my kitchen. I had to secure the flour and sugar and such. I don't remember how we got rid of them.

I had been walking with the kids and got back to the house and there was a big snake coiled at the front door. Somehow I called a neighbor, an elderly lady who came over and killed it with a hoe.

One more near catastrophe. I was cleaning in the kitchen and had thrown an empty egg carton on the floor. We had open gas heaters. Chuck put the carton in the fire and put it on our bed. When I saw it, the bed was on fire. Somehow I got it out, but the feather bed was ruined and a very pretty Dutch doll quilt Mother had made us. I am glad that was all the damage.

That bed was propped up. Jerry had stacked some family Bibles he was selling to prop up the bed. We were sleeping on the Word.

The church members loved us and we loved them. Karen was born there in 1967. Sister Mable put a baby bed in the sanctuary to relieve me so I could take part in the service. We have fond memories of her family as well as Brother Tommy and Sister Dot.

1967 was the Six-Day war in Israel. Israel took the West Bank from Jordan, the Gaza Strip from Egypt, and the Golan Heights from Syria. I remember Brother Arthur, a church member, said we are in the days of "When you see these things coming, look up. Your redemption draweth nigh." He thought this was pretty significant.

After two years, we were appointed to a different church- to Picayune near the Gulf Coast. Another group of faithful members: Brother Hammonds, Sister Julie, Sister Hollis and families. Jerry worked for Gordon Jewelers, and I hired a lady to come cook and watch the children, and I taught a year of eighth grade in Picayune. I love to tell this story. We were studying "The Courtship of Miles Standish" by Longfellow. The selection was in our book and we were all into this when one of my students said, "Mrs. Cook, I am related to Miles Standish." I was taken aback, but he continued, and said his family had a book that someone in his genealogy line had put together and I could read it. I made notes from the book and wrote down the line that Gary came from. He was eleven generations from the Captain. I got the biggest kick out of that.

Miles Standish, who had served in the army in England, was part of the group of merchants, craftsmen, and indentured servants going to America on the Mayflower. In other words, the passengers on the Mayflower were not all Separatist Pilgrims desiring religious liberty.

Let's take a look at the Separatist group on the Mayflower fleeing religious persecution. Henry VIII had cut ties with the Roman Catholic Church. He replaced the pope as head and changed the name to the Church of England, but it was still a catholic church. The Separatists wanted to separate from the church that still followed the rituals and traditions of the Roman church that they said were not in the Bible. They were persecuted for their beliefs.

A group of Separatists first went to Holland but later took passage on the Mayflower in 1620 and settled in the New World, meaning to land in Virginia, but landed further north in Cape Cod. So, they were free to set up their own self-government in the new Plymouth Colony. Their Mayflower Compact was a precedent the founding fathers later followed when writing the Constitution. Pretty heavy stuff.

The other group of dissidents were the Puritans who wanted to purify the Church of England. They came in 1630 and formed the Massachusetts Bay Colony, the predecessor of several colonies in Massachusetts Bay. They set up schools so the children could learn to read the Bible. Harvard College was a Puritan college, named after a Puritan from Boston, John Harvard.

Hurricane Camille hit the Mississippi Gulf coast while we lived in Picayune. We had gone to perform a wedding at Spanish Fort when it hit. We just drove on up to Charleston and stayed a week but then decided to go back home to Picayune. Trees were down on the roadside as we made our way south. In Picayune, the power was still out. Families got together and cooked up foods from the freezers on a gas stove to keep the food from going bad.

At the end of the pastorate and the school year, we moved back to Paynes, a community near Charleston, and started sixteen years of living on Cole Hill, sharing the old farmhouse with Bessie and Jesse Cole, Jerry's grandparents.

I taught at Paynes Academy. Connie was born. Bessie took care of the new baby and Kenny and Karen. Chuck started first grade.

Bessie and Jesse were Jerry's grandparents but were parents to all of us. They took care of us. Jesse raised fields of peas and corn, sweet potatoes, Irish potatoes, peanuts, watermelons, tomatoes, and had a garden of mustard, lettuce, cabbage, carrots, beets, cucumbers, radishes, onions, butterbeans, green beans, squash, and okra. He mostly gathered the produce. Bessie put it up and cooked it.

The first appliance Jerry and I bought was a deep freezer. I loved freezing and canning the vegetables. And we had apples, peaches, black berries, plums, muscadines as well.

I put up soup mix, chow chow, homemade tomato ketchup, pickled beets, green beans, black berry jam. Plus filled the freezer.

We also bought a wood heater that sat in front of the fireplace. It certainly put out the heat whereas a fireplace only warms one side of you. One side is too hot and the other side is freezing. Anyone remember that? Jesse would keep the fire going during the day while we were at work. Bessie would put my washed laundry in the dryer for me and also share her leftovers with us for supper. Those two could work all day and do a three-week revival at night and not skip a beat. Jesse still ploughed with a mule. You could hear him in the field giving that stubborn mule what for.

The barn was just across the road from the house. That is where the pigs were kept. The school bus climbed the hill and stopped right in front of the barn. All the kids on the bus would hold their noses. Jesse would do a hog killing in the back yard. There would be pork chops, ribs, sausage, chitterlings.

Bessie and Jesse eventually put up with four teenagers. They were patient, but it was not easy. The farm house had been partitioned down the middle and two kitchens added on the back, with ONE BATH in between. So there were like two separate apartments with the one bath on the back of the house in the middle for them and for us. Bessie and Jesse would keep a chamber pot under their bed at night if the bathroom door to their side of the house got locked. Jesse put up with Chuck and Kenny. They would hide in a tree by the barn. Jesse would come through with the mule. He would tell the mule to go. They would tell it to stop.

We all put up with Chuck playing his drums so loud you could hear them into next week. At one time Chuck and Kenny were part of a family of Kilgore sisters that sang gospel songs. Kenny played the bass guitar for them, and Chuck played the drums. Those ladies loved those boys.

My kids loved growing up out on those eighty acres in the Paynes community. The boys had guns and hunted deer, rabbit, or doves. They sometimes camped out. They swung on the kudzu vines. I know the boys went down to a neighbor's pond and swam in that dirty water.

Once when Kenny was six or seven, he went to the woods where Jerry and others were cutting wood. Somehow they left before he got there. It was dark and he was lost. He remembered Jerry told him to follow the pipeline. He did and came out at the highway. A neighbor brought him home. He was a smart little bugger.

I have another memory of him at that age. Jerry was holding a revival and Kenny went down to the altar for salvation. There he was. I looked down and he was barefooted as a goose. I had to wonder what a certain visitor thought. Kenny remembers on my 36th birthday he saved up nickels and dimes and put them in a coffee can to give me on my birthday. He had saved $36.00.

When the kids were young, someone came by selling books, the <u>Children's Family Library</u>. Ten volumes of Bible stories, nice pictures, and very scholarly presented. I would gather my kids around me and read the Old Testament stories to them. I did not have that $40.00 to spare, but those books became very basic to a lot of my church work.

Chuck reminded me of some of the shenanigans the four of them got into. Once we adults were at church and the kids were at home by themselves. It was night. They saw lights flickering on and off down the hill by the pond. They started imagining that someone was signaling to someone on the hill and maybe they were up to no good, a break-in or something. They were scared and imagined more and got more scared. Chuck unloaded a round of BB shot toward the lights but no one said, 'Don't shoot," and they kept flickering. Karen put Connie, scared and crying, in a room to protect her and went to talk to the boys. Then she went back, hunched over closer to the floor in case anyone was at the window. When she got to Connie, it scared her. She threw her arms out, hands braced. Her arms were trembling and she was backing up and stuttering," Nooooooooo!" When the adults got home, Chuck and Kenny took a light and went down to investigate. A tree sapling had fallen over on the electric fence and was shorting it out. They love to tell this and get hilariously tickled when they do.

Karen reminded me of the time the boys went camping with their Uncle Barry. They heard a bunch of coyotes howling. Barry charged off with a gun to shoot them. He turned around to see if Chuck and Kenny were with him. They had high-tailed it to the top of the van!

Kenny reminded me of tornado scares. We would all run down and try to avoid getting all muddy in a ditch. In Florida, we run from the hurricanes. The whole top of one tree fell in the yard. Another one leaned against the house, another one cracked and lay across the neighbor's roof with no damage. Tree surgeons then take advantage. They charge an arm and a leg.

During those years, Jerry, no longer involved in church work, drove an eighteen wheeler for Kimco, transporting auto parts across country. He also worked in law enforcement, retiring years later as a tactical commander at the Parchman Correctional Facility. I taught at Strider, a private school. The yearbook staff dedicated the 1973 yearbook to me.

We went to church at Adams Arbor, an old established church with a good-sized congregation. I worked with the Children's Church program along with Yvonne Winters, Henrece Murphy, Clara Tartt, Bett Osbarn, Linda Todd, and Edwina Newsom. I wrote plays and we presented them in church. I wrote a Joseph play from a Joseph comic book. Clara made Kenny a coat of many colors. The name of the play was, "Am I my Brother's Keeper?" Yvonne and I worked closely together in Children's Church. Our kids were: Stephen and Vicki, Rodney, Tammy and Joey, Mona, Christy and Amanda, Bob and Alicia, Jason, Lyndell, Pam, Kim, Chuck, Kenny, Karen and Connie.

I wrote puppet skits. One time Chuck adlibbed during the skit. He was so funny I couldn't sleep that night for laughing. Connie was in a play one time. "Connie, do you remember there was a bird in a cage that answered to one of your lines?" Jason and Vicki were in a skit. He was grandpa reading a newspaper. Grandma told him to move his feet. She was cleaning. He threw up his legs and his house shoes flew way up in the air. "Kim, do you remember you forgot your line and sputtered, 'That turkey is still…tough!' Alicia and Amanda remember dancing in red tutus.

Connie, Mona, Joey, Stephen, and Vicki

Amanda

I wrote an Esther play. Karen was Esther. A lady from India lent us saris for the girls' costumes. We tied the curtains together to form the columns for a palace. The kids did great with their parts. I remember going home. I sat on the bed and just was overwhelmed with the feeling that God was sitting there by me and he said, "Well, we did it, didn't we?" He was saying, "Well, we pulled it off, you and I." I will never forget that sense of him being so approachable and sitting there talking to me like another person.

Brother Kroon was our pastor. His sermons were original, anointed, and God many times would visit the service. He would like just walk in and you would know He was there. His presence was real. I helped Brother Kroon write a book. To show his appreciation, he gave us a little girl's playhouse he had built to sell, but somebody stole the Snoopy off the top. Nothing but the ears laying out flat on the roof. Connie loved that playhouse. I would look out the kitchen window and see her teaching her dolls and laying it off to them how they better act.

Karen and Connie

Brother Wilkerson followed Brother Kroon. He had a good singing ministry. Brother Wilkerson was a big worker in the Youth Camp. I was asked to provide a theme and decorate for the camp one year. We did a Western theme. I scoured the town for anything for atmosphere. One person lent me cow head skeletons. Sometimes I would play and sing for small weddings for church members.

After that I became really good friends with Edwardanne McCammon and attended prayer groups with her in town and out of town. The speakers ministered and operated in the gifts. I began to see worship in operation rather than just praise. It was another special time of enlightenment on my journey.

In my teaching career of forty-one years, I taught 6th, 7th, 8th English, English I, II, III, and IV. French I and II. In 1975, I left Strider and went to town to teach at Charleston High School. I was the co-sponsor of the National Honor Society with Linda Lewis. We had induction ceremonies for the students who were eligible academically and possessed good character. We sponsored a Gong Show for the public. My French Club sponsored a fashion show in the school auditorium named for Morgan Freeman who lives in Charleston.

Chuck and Kenny

Under the direction and Mr. Micou, my children were all in the Charleston High School Band. I worked in the concession stand at the games, bought the food for hamburgers and hotdogs. Alice Clolinger and other band boosters helped and the proceeds went to the band. Alice was my hairdresser and my good friend and confidant.

Karen enjoyed high school. She was a cheerleader and on the homecoming court.

Christmas was lots of family, food, and opening gifts. We had Christmas at my mother's with me and Jerry and kids, Jim and Macki and Missy, David and Vicki and Cindy, Laura Kathryn and Merideth, at my Aunt Virginia's with Kit and Annette and Mike and Sharon and their families, at Nita's with Jerry and me, Barry, Roger, Ricky, and families. My kids grew up with their grandparents and cousins. It is sad we are scattered.

Karen, Jerry, Chuck, Marilyn, Kenny, and Connie

We never had money to eat out or go on a vacation. My uncle took us to the Shepherd of the Hills country in the Ozarks when I was a child. My brother, Jim, took the kids and me to Branson, Missouri, also to the Nutcracker in Memphis, and to Elvis Presley's house. Another time he took my mother, her sister, Virginia, and me to the Natchez Pilgrimage. We saw the stately antebellum homes and there was the Pageant with music, dance, and costumes that reflected the Old South. Later in life, I got a chance to go places and experience other cultures, but that would come later, after a divorce and a move to Florida.

My daddy died before my boys joined the Navy. He was Navy, so he would have liked that. In 1984 and 1985, Chuck and Kenny did basic training in Great Lakes, and both would be stationed at Cecil Field in Jacksonville. Karen planned to marry. Connie and I would move to Florida.

Life in the Sunshine State

1986-1997

Florida, England trip, and Colorado

So, here is how this came about. Cecil Allison, who was raised in the cotton fields of Tippo, Mississippi, made his teaching career in Jacksonville, Florida. He could have you in stitches telling how he told his dad he didn't want to be a farmer. Dr. Allison was a card, very intelligent and always reaching out to help people, but he came across as hilariously funny. He could have been a stand-up comedian.

In 1986, his aunt died, my mother's neighbor, in Charleston. He ordered flowers from my mother who was a florist. He asked about me. She said, "Marilyn is teaching here. She has two sons in the Navy in Jacksonville." He said, "Tell her if she wants to come here, I can get her a job, and she will have a better retirement."

I waffled a while, not wanting to go so far and leave my mother, and start a new life at age 47. Edwardanne took me to Jacksonville to apply for the job. We stayed with Chuck who had married. Back home for Karen's wedding. Soon after, Connie and I left the hill with my brother, David, driving a moving truck with all our possessions, driving all night. The Allisons helped me find an apartment on the Westside where my school, Joseph Stilwell, was located and also the church that the boys attended.

Kenny was on deployment with the Forrestal when we got to Jacksonville. What fun it was when they got back and came into port, all in uniform and lining the entire deck. Boy, the excitement when the ship comes in and the guys get home. It wasn't long after, he married, and not long after, grandkids from the three marriages started arriving.

Florida students were different from the kids in Mississippi. Maybe more exposed to life. I can't say. They were products of a big city and theme parks, travel, more sure of themselves. The school system was more progressive. That first year was a time of adjustment. Connie attended Forest High School in the 10th grade. I am sure she had an adjustment as well.

I taught at Stilwell four years. Some wonderful friends: Susan Rhoten Jones, Joanne Philpot, Joyce Davidson, Frances Young, Anne Inman, Betsey O'Donnell. I was nominated and inducted into the Delta Kappa Gamma Society. During spring break of 1990, I got to do a Cosmos trip to Europe with Rosemary Buie, one of my colleagues. To London, across the channel, Paris, France, the Benelux countries, Belgium, Holland, Germany, the Rhine, the cathedrals. I dearly loved it.

But my world would come crashing in. I was surplused, meaning the enrollment dropped at Stilwell, and being the last English teacher hired, I was sent to Jean Ribault on the Northside. With the Persian Gulf crisis, Chuck was sent to the Gulf on the John F. Kennedy. I am covered up in an Inner City school and culture. He works on the flight deck at night in a war. Not the best of worlds.

But he got home safely (to New Jersey), and I learned to love and have success with my students. I am tempted to add a little local color.

To the south of here is Cross Creek. This is the scrub country that Marjorie Rawlings fell in love with and the inspiration for her writing, especially <u>The Yearling</u>. I have been to the house, orange groves, palmetto woods twice, and soaked up her story and showed the movie to my students many times. Gregory Peck and Jane Wyman do justice to the story and the little boy Jody with his fawn- it is classic.

Tying in with our studies, I loved to show that movie and also <u>Oliver Twist</u> with George C. Scott as Fagin. <u>Heidi</u> with Sir Michael Redgrave as grandfather, <u>The Odyssey</u> with Armand Assante as Ulysses, <u>A Tale of Two Cities</u> with Chris Sarandon as Charles Darnay and Sydney Carton. Totally amazing movies. Wonderful substance, actors, drama.

In 1994, I met Betsy Smith at St Peters Episcopal Church and we roomed together at a women's retreat at Epworth by the Sea. This is a Methodist conference facility. John Wesley was from Epworth, England.

We became friends. She had joined a group called Friendship Force which is an organization whose focus is to promote peace between countries by having people travel to other countries, stay in homes, and form friendships. There was a trip to England planned that summer. I knew I wanted to go.

I joined Friendship Force, and Betsy Smith and I, Carole Phillips, Bob, and Todd went from Jacksonville. I cannot communicate how wonderful it was. I stayed the first week in Loughborough in the Midlands with Roy and Dorothy Cope. They showed me so much love and took me out in the English countryside with the cows and sheep and dry wall fences and the English churches and graveyards. They took me to Anne Hathaway's house and Shakespeare's. The Avon River. Leicester Market. Driving on the other side of the road was strange and it was the first time I saw roundabouts.
One of the group's activities was bowling. They called it skittles. We had teams and tried our luck at knocking the pins down. The

British are so full of themselves. They kept up a constant dialogue cheering and groaning in unison for the players. They are insanely funny. We had a garden party at Judy's. We met Lichfield Morris dancers. At the farewell party, everyone danced- Roy and Dorothy so graceful gliding across the floor. Jean singing Edelweiss. I am crying. Roy had a silly monkey puppet he was cutting up with. I danced with him and nearly fell when he twirled me around and we fell out laughing.

Roy and Dorothy had a little cottage they named Killiecrankie (named after a battle fought in Scotland). His garden of roses was so beautiful. He got awards each year for the explosion of roses in the front yard. I became a devoted Anglophile.

I wrote a poem, borrowing the first stanza, continuing with my words.

> "Our England is a garden that is full of stately views,
> Of borders, beds, and shrubberies and lawns and avenues."
> --- Robert Louis Stevenson

> Of black-faced sheep on hillsides, fenced with quarried stones
> Curtained cottages in villages and cups of tea and scones.
> Our England is a study of yellow fields and red
> Cathedral spires and castles where monks and knights once tread.
> What a sense of antiquity!
> The houses of uniformity, whether stone or timbered
> Explosion of color!
> In terraces, lanes and streets, at angles, on slopes
> Set in hills and dales, all so quaint
> And laid out with careful planning,
> And every burgeoning blossom eagerly anticipated.

England is a celebration of our faith, history, and heritage,
>And a celebration of loveliness.
>I will remember that awesome loveliness,
>And the people who showed me warmth and love."

Well, Denis Hickling picked us up and rode with us to our second week up in Newcastle upon Tyne. I cried the whole trip. I have never bonded with anyone like I did Roy and Dorothy.

I was in for another treat. Ann Asch hosted me the second week. She lived in Hexham and was working, but she had a fabulous weekend planned and also took off one day and drove us to Edinburgh. What a treat. We did the bus around the city and then did it again. Edinburgh Castle, Robert Burn's statue, David Livingston's, Sir Walter Scott's statue, John Knox's house.

In Northumbria I went with the group to Alnwick Castle, Craster, (a fishing village), the Lake District (Wordsworth country). Ann took me to Tynemouth Castle and Priory, Hadrian's Wall, Washington Old Hall, (the home of George Washington's ancestors). We went to Durham Cathedral and there was the Venerable Bede's crypt! I read about him in college but never dreamed our paths would cross. I stood there thinking, "There is no way I am standing by the crypt of the Venerable Bede." We did a Shakespeare on the lawn.

Ann lives in Hexham. When you are approaching Hexham, the Abbey is sitting high on a hill and is lit up at night. It is so beautiful and commanding. It is austere.

We flew home to Florida. That was the first time I had met Carole and we became the best of friends until this day, a beautiful, intelligent, spiritual, interesting, and personable lady.

Betsy Smith opened up two venues for me. She told me more about Dale Howard who pastored an Episcopal church in the Arlington area in Jacksonville. And she told me more about Eugenia Price who wrote historical novels along the East Coast. There is the Savannah quartet, the St. Simons trilogy, and the Florida trilogy. I became so enamored of her stories. The history is exciting, the characters real, and her faith inspiring.

Betsey O'Donnell, Joanne Philpot, and I made a trip to Savannah, GA., because we were all into Eugenia Price's stories, specifically <u>Don Juan McQueen</u>. Both my friends had babies in strollers. We went to a cemetery to try and find Don Juan McQueen's wife's gravesite. They were slow, so I walked on ahead and walked straight to the grave across a large cemetery. I started squealing. It was surreal. The book is heart-wrenching, Anne preferring safe, Protestant Savannah. Don Juan totally captivated by dangerous, Spanish, Catholic East Florida.

I have been to Anson Dodge's church in Fernandina on St. Simons many times and taken friends there as well to see Christ Church Frederica and cemetery with the giant live oak trees draped in fairytale Spanish moss and his grave and the family plot. <u>Beloved Invader</u> is a love story and more than that. It is as captivating as is St. Simons itself.

I have been to Hibernia and taken friends there to Margaret's church and the family plot. The novel, <u>Margaret's Story</u>, is set in the Civil War on "their river", the mighty St. Johns. Another gut-wrenching story of love and faith.

As far as Dale Howard and his ministry, he and others pulled out of the Episcopal Church USA. He started a church on Arlington Expressway, a local Charismatic Episcopal Church which was becoming pretty well-known across the world. It was a convergence worship: the basic fundamental salvation message, liturgy, and the spirit-filled Charismatic stream; other words, the basic Protestant teaching, the Anglican liturgy, and the Pentecostal experience combined. Connie and I moved to apartments in Arlington, and we started attending that church. We soon felt comfortable and I think grew in our spiritual walk.

In 1996 another travel opportunity came about. Our Friendship Force chapter in Jacksonville was going to Colorado. They had gone with us to England in 1994. Carole was the exchange director. I decided to go.

The Colorado chapter was in Grand Junction. The Welcome Party featured square dancing. We tried to participate, me and Carole laughing with our "two left feet". This was my first experience in the West. We drove around in the Colorado Monument which is breath-taking.

We loved Fort Uncompahgre, a reconstructed fur-trading post. Trappers traded furs for guns, tools, food stuffs. The guides showed us how you scrape the pelt to make the beaver hats which were sent to England. The pelt was boiled, dried, and rubbed with mercury. Mercury affects the nervous system so people who did this a lot could become mentally deficient, thus the phrase "mad-hatter"! Beaver hats were expensive, maybe a month's salary for a hat. I do know the beaver trade drove the trapping industry.

We did the Arches National Park in Utah. We attended a Pow Wow. We went white water rafting.

But Ouray I will always remember. It is nestled in a valley with mountains towering above. Imagine waking up every morning and looking up at the mountains dotted with trees and finally snow-capped, like sentinels jutting into blue sky and white cloud puffs. This Is the sky line you look up and see hovering over the quaint buildings in the town on all sides, because the town sits in the valley surrounded by mountains.

We planned some entertainment for the group. I had written the lyrics for a song high-lighting our trip. They were to the tune of "The Red River Valley". We sang it for our hosts.

> "Well, we came to say hello from River City
> As you know we have come a long way

Just to visit our friends in Colorado
Whom we've known ever since that fine day
When we visited England together
Beer and skittles, and good vittles, cups of tea
Ancient castles, cathedrals, and people
Took us back into time and history."

"We have had so much fun in Grand Junction
Red rock canyons, mesa cliffs, sand stone spires
Tyrannosaurus Rex, you were next on our agenda
Castle Valley, Dead Horse Point, open skies.

Since we know we have formed many friendships,
There will be a few tears in our eyes
For it's time for us to leave Colorado
And it's time for us to say our good byes."

I hesitated to go on that trip, but I am so glad I went.

Our Jacksonville Friendship Force chapter has had incoming exchanges as well as outgoing. I have hosted a couple from Utah, a couple from the Netherlands, and the exchange director from Irkutsk, Siberia. I cherish the gifts they brought, including beautiful picture books.

I got to know Louise Daniels on the Colorado exchange. In May of 1997, Louise and I went to the Spoleto Arts Festival in historic Charleston, SC. We saw a lady do a dramatic monologue impersonating Mary Boykin Chestnut, a famous diarist of the Civil War. Her husband was advisor to Jefferson Davis. The performance was excellent as is the diary. There is a very good tour of Ft. Sumter. In 1861, the Confederates fired on this Union garrison, the first shots fired in the Civil War. Mary's husband, James Chestnut, delivered Beauregard's final command to Major Anderson prior to the bombardment of Ft. Sumter.

We also heard the "Fourth Day" Singers do beautiful phrase and worship music at one of the churches. They gave me a tape I have played over and over. After that, Louise set it up for me to attend a Walk to Emmaus. This is the Methodist version of the Catholic Cursillo, which is a three-day weekend to train Christian leaders. The "Fourth Day" represents living out the rest of your life after the intense weekend. She contacted my family and friends unbeknown to me. At the end of the conference, everyone opens letters that family and friends have written to you. I have all of these and would not take anything for them. Especially one from my mother and my sister-in-law, Vicki.

I want to include Melissa Erickson in my story. She was my hairdresser for years. I could share my trips and up's and down's with her. She is one of the few who could do wonders with my hair. She and John have nine children she homeschools. She is awesome.

And then, my first adventure with YWAM.

YWAM Harpenden/England, and Germany/Austria

1997-2002

My youngest daughter, Connie, married in 1997. They married in a castle near St. Augustine. She and I put together a video with the wedding pictures and a sound track of Camelot. She was beautiful. The castle was romantic. What can you say? They soon moved to Ft. Campbell, Kentucky, in the army.

I visited family many times through the years. In 1997 and 1998, I flew a total of eight times.

At the Episcopal Church in 1998, I met a lady who was able to stop teaching and go full time into ministry with YWAM. I could not do that; she told me people could volunteer to work on a short term basis for YWAM. She gave me the address of the base in England. I contacted Jennifer Page and arranged to go in the summer as a mission builder for three weeks at the Harpenden base.

YWAM stands for Youth with a Mission. It is a mission organization worldwide that allows young people to be trained in the Father Heart of God at one of the bases and then go on outreach to minister in mostly third world countries. I arrived at the base in Harpenden, just north of London, for a three week volunteer work assignment. My job was to help in the kitchen under the supervision of Anne Nicholson. Anne is a Cordon Bleu cook. She could plan the most colorful, appetizing dishes. The students taking courses and the staff who ate in the cafeteria were blessed.

I had another agenda while I was there. On the weekends I would walk down to the train station and take the train to Victoria Station in London and do daytrips on Saturdays and Sundays. I went to Windsor Castle and Hampton Court. I went to Leeds Castle, the white cliffs of Dover, Canterbury Cathedral where Thomas Beckett was martyred. This was the destination of Chaucer's pilgrims in <u>The Canterbury Tales</u>. The movie, <u>Beckett</u>, with Richard Burton and Peter O'Toole is absolutely classic. I went to the Cotswolds, where hamlets built of local limestone of a warm yellow color, nestle in the countryside. I went to Blenheim Palace, the birthplace of Winston Churchill, to Covent Garden, and to an evensong at St. Paul's Cathedral. I did a tour of London. I went to Westminster Abbey, the Royal Albert Hall, cruise on the Thames, the Tower of London, Bath, Stonehenge, Salisbury Cathedral, Cambridge.

PBS aired the musical <u>Les Miserables</u> from the Royal Albert featuring Colm Wilkinson as Jean Valjean. His performance- well you just are carried to an epiphany of emotion. And then after the performance, all the men who have played Jean Valjean in other countries come down the aisle with their country's flag and take the stage, each one singing solo, in their language, creating a medley of the theme song from the musical. I don't have words for it. Absolutely sensational.

I thoroughly enjoyed my life with friends in my lodging at the mission base; knowing Anne Nicholson was a wonderful treat. Years later, Anne came and worked with a church ministry in Atlanta. I drove up to see her, and later she drove down to Jacksonville to visit me.

At the end of three weeks at the mission base, I left Harpenden and took a train up to visit Ann Asch in Northumberland whom I met in Friendship Force in 1994. I got off at York and walked around, saw the York Minster, back on train to Corbridge. She had moved from Hexham to Corbridge. This second visit with Ann was a sequel to two things. She had sent me a book in 1996 that whetted my interest in Lindisfarne. I was intrigued. So we went. It is a holy island, part of the cradle of the Celtic church. Oswald, a Christian king in Northumberland, sent for help to evangelize his people. Aidan came and founded Lindisfarne, a monastic community. Cuthbert preached there. In 793 AD., the Vikings raided Lindisfarne. Only a few monks escaped. I love reading about the Celtic persuasion which was different from the Roman Church.

So, after reading extensively about Lindisfarne, I got to go in 1998. The other thing is when we were in England before, in 1994, with Friendship Force, and went to the Lake District, the tour bus passed by Wordsworth's house, Dove Cottage. Just kept going. When I saw this I am thinking, "No way. Wordsworth, the Romantic poet I was in love with in college. There's his house- I can see it out the window and we are just going to go on down the road. Surely you are stopping!" But we didn't stop. So this trip, 1998, Ann took me to the Lake District and dropped me off. I stayed in a wonderful bed and breakfast and I went to Dove Cottage and did the tour. I also heard readings of Wordsworth's poems at St. Oswald's Church in Grasmere and got to see Wordsworth's grave there. I guess that is closure.

I was so happy years later when Ann Asch and her brother and sister came to St. Augustine. I drove down and got to visit with them.

I took a train on to Loughborough to see Roy and Dorothy again. This time we went to a bell foundry to watch them cast a bell. To a carillon and climbed to the top and watched the man working a big keyboard to ring the bells. To a museum in Quorn with military artifacts. Roy was in the Normandy Invasion. He shared his story.

The first time I visited Roy and Dorothy in 1994, we went to Bradgate Park where Lady Jane Grey's family lived. She was queen of England for nine days after Henry VIII's son died. When I got back home, I became obsessed with the Lady Jane movie, a tragic love story and a stark reality of the horror that the Protestant Reformation brought into being, with Catholics and Protestants killing one another. However, I personally believe it was necessary-- what Luther taught. "Sola scripture", scripture only is the way to salvation, not church tradition.

Lady Jane's story is moving. My second visit in 1998 to Bradgate Park we went to the ruins of her parents' house and thoroughly enjoyed the tour guide. He knew the history of the family who mistreated Jane, who arranged a marriage that put her on the throne for nine days, and turned their back when things went down. She was not in line for the throne. She was innocent in a political plot. Mary, the daughter of Henry VIII by Catherine of Aragon, his first wife, was in line. Her supporters rose up and demanded she have the throne. Jane was accused of treason, taken to the tower and beheaded.

After Bloody Mary's rule, Elizabeth I ruled, but had no heirs. Mary, Queen of Scots was in line but very Catholic. Charges were trumped up against her because England wanted to remain Protestant and avoid another Catholic monarch, so Mary, Queen of Scots, was accused of plotting against Elizabeth and put to death. With Mary taken out, her son James who was non-committal in church persuasions, was in line for the throne, James I.

The summer of 1999 we had a family reunion with Jerry, myself, our four children and grandchildren. We had get-togethers at Grenada Dam and David and Vicki's. Our family included Chuck and Holly, Chuck's girls: Kaley and Darla. Kenny and Sandy, their children: Jennifer, Justin and Tyler. Karen and Carl, Karen's children: Jacob and Jessica. Zoey Beth came later. Chris and Connie, their son: Samuel. Synjon came later.

I bought a house in Jacksonville in 2000 and was just moving in when my mother died July 4. The date was kind of fitting since Jefferson and Adams also died July 4. She loved history as I do. My mother had built a nice florist business later in life. She was artistic and created nice arrangements. She also took up painting. I am proud of some of her paintings and enjoy her quilts. She and my grandmother were seamstresses and quilters, gardeners and good cooks. My brothers and I thank her for her hard work and raising us to be God-fearing and productive people. I want to thank Linda VanderPoel, who works at the Extended Care where my mother lived for years, for being a blessing to the residents.

In 2001, I arranged a party for Charlestonians who live in Jacksonville. Dr. Cecil Allison and Peggy came. Vivian Tribble Welch and Bill. Dan L. Fedric and Kay. Carolyn James Hartman and Charlie. Catherine, Don, and Skylar.

In 2001, I got a transfer to Jefferson Davis Middle School. That was the year of 9/11. We were in second period when we got the news the towers were hit. We all know America has not been the same, especially with the wars that followed. Afghanistan, Iraq, and now Syria. The Middle East in chaos. Refugee crisis. Susan Rhoten Jones, my long-time friend from Stilwell, put in a word for me to get the transfer. She was then at Jeff Davis. Soon I was friends with Susan Santos , Carol Smith, Jane Bowman, Regina Manning, Mary Saffer.

By now, my grandchildren count was up to ten, and as I write this in 2017, the great grands' count is six. The great grands are: Cayden, Charlotte, Aurora, Brindle, Lakota, and Ginny. Well, life moves along and another trip became possible.

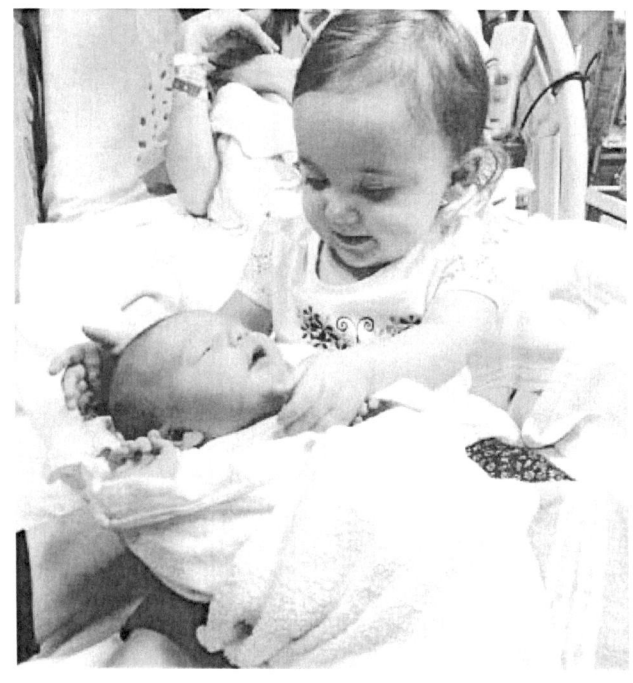

Brindle and Lakota

In 2002, I was able to go to Germany and Austria. In Germany I had a cousin who is a doctor/professor in the Department of Chemistry at Johns Hopkins University in Baltimore, MD. Kit Bowen would go to Munich a lot in connection with his position. I visited him and Annette. One of the first places I saw was the Rathaus (pronounced rat house) in Munich. I think it is the identifying mark of Marienplatz which takes its name from Mary, the patron saint of Bavaria. It is a large, several-storied building with red flowers in flower pots all across the front. It took my breath away.

We went to the Englischer Garden, a famous beer garden. And of course everyone's must-see is the Hofbrauhaus, the famous beer hall. So full of camaraderie, beer drinkers, good food, and German music. I bought a CD. Kit took us to the Weiskirke church, so beautiful. I've never seen such an ornate pink, blue, white and gold wonder. We ate at Augustiner House, a Bratwurst sausage, kraut, a very good sweet mustard. We ate at the Viktualienmarkt. We drove to Oberammergau, where the Passion Play is performed every ten years to thank God for sparing the village from the plague. Once, walking down a street, Kit pointed out where Hitler led a march before his rise to power. We went to Chiemsee built by King Ludwig II. They had just been to Neuschwanstein Castle so I missed that.

Time for the second leg of my trip. I took a train to Vienna to visit a girl I hosted nine years before with People to People. Annette Kaneider had since married Thomas Schubert and they continued the wonderful hosting my cousin's family provided. We went to a restaurant called Heurigen. It means "this year's wine". Thomas took me to Shonbrunn Palace, a symbol of the greatness of the former Imperial Austria. Maria Theresa was Empress of the Habsburg Dynasty. She and her husband and sixteen children lived at Shonbrunn. Marie-Antoinette was one of their daughters.

Kennedy and Khrushchev met in 1961 at Shonbrunn to come to an agreement on Arms Control.

Annette served wonderful meals: Hungarian goulash, and a tasty tuna spread on brown bread. Austrian bread is to die for. She made a bread dumpling cooked in a towel that was interesting, a tasty cucumber salad. Wine. We would have homemade preserves. Her mother had apple, apricot, pear, and peach trees in their yard. Once we ate at a Chinese place. I had crispy duck, deep-fried, served on a bed of bean sprouts, leeks, onion, carrots. Served with rice and a syrupy soy sauce.

We did a walking tour of Vienna, whose buildings are Gothic and Baroque structures, the music capital of the world. We saw the Strauss and Mozart memorials. We would see two-headed eagles on monuments, representing the Austria-Hungary Empire up until WWI. The monarch in Austria was automatically the monarch of Hungary.

We drove to Burgenland on the Hungarian border. The houses were interesting. Very large rounded doors because they used to roll whole wagons into an open hallway inside the house loaded with produce. Inside they would make wine, shuck corn, weave baskets. I remember the stork nests on top of roofs.

We visited her parents. The house has Persian rugs, beautiful tile on the floors extending very high up the walls. I thought it was elegant. We went to their church (no one there) and climbed up a flight of old steps where the organ is, and Annette played, and we sang " Silent Night" together which was written in Austria. The story goes that in Oberndorf, people were meeting for church. The organ was broken. Two people in the service wrote the piece during the meeting and it was played and sung to guitar accompaniment. Then, back at their home, Annette played and her father sang. So fun, and then she played Strauss waltzes.

Thomas shared a lot of Austrian history with me and just so much knowledge in general. Two things I remember. He loved the prestige that Old Austria had before WWI. He bought me a lapel pin of Old Austria. Another thing I grasped was how significant the founding of America was. All of Europe always had monarchies. That was really a big thing to set up the country that our founding fathers envisioned. I had never really made that connection. And I didn't know the Ottoman Empire and the Habsburg Dynasty ended with WWI.

I really would like to mention my theory about WWI. In England, Queen Victoria and Albert had nine children. Vicky, the oldest, married the German Kaiser. Their son was Kaiser Wilhelm II who ruled from 1888-1918, during WWI. Victoria and Albert's oldest son was Edward VII, (called Bertie) who ruled 1901-1910. Wilhelm was jealous of his Uncle Bertie and his British Navy and his rapport with the European countries. Wilhelm built a large German Navy to keep up with Britain. Wilhelm was cruel to his British mother. He was full of German nationalism from a child.

When a Serbian nationalist assassinated the Arch Duke of Austria in 1914, Austria waited to declare war until they knew they had Germany's backing which they got. Then the other countries took sides. Wilhelm enjoyed his position of power. I cannot help but wonder how much the war's escalating depended on him?

Just to continue the interesting marriages of Victoria and Albert's children: First, Bertie (Edward VII) married Alexandra from Denmark. Her sister Dagmar married the Tsar of Russia. Their son was Nicholas II, Tsar of Russia (1894-1917). One of Victoria and Albert's daughters was Alice, whose daughter was Alexandra (Alix) who married Nicholas II. They and their children were killed by the Bolsheviks. I wonder why England did not give them asylum.

I said my good-byes to Annette and family and took a train to Salzburg, Austria, now on my own. Salzburg is built on the Salzach River with the Hohensalzburg Fortress so elevated it is visible from anywhere in the city. It dominates the skyline.

I took a tour of the salt mines. At one time salt was used for trading. One pound of salt equaled one pound of gold. It was a precious commodity. The soldiers were paid in salt. The word 'salary' comes from the same root word for salt. We got to the mine. My tour guide and I sat on a long slide, me holding around her waist and us holding our feet up and Whoosh! We went down the chute. We walked along the tracks of the mining cars. We were told how the salt was mined and what it was used for. While underground we crossed the border to Germany and back again. Austria is a land-locked country, no sea salt, so this area was a great source of salt.

We went to a reconstructed Celtic village. There was a reproduction of a red-headed witch. Witch hunts were common. They were kept in hanging copper containers. If they touched the ground they might disappear.

I walked to Getreidegasse Street and went to Mozart's birthplace. He was born in 1756 and performing in 1761. His father recognized his son's genius. Mozart played for church services, for royal entertainment. He composed. There were no copyright laws. His father was careful not to let original scores out of his hands of Mozart's music.

I attended a dinner theater and a "Sound of Music" show. A four-course dinner and piano (Viennese waltzes) followed by five performers who sang songs from the movie, then a clip of Maria Von Trapp telling about marrying the Captain. As we know from the movie, the Von Trapp family was forced to leave Austria in 1938 when Hitler announced the Anschluss, the union of Austria and Germany.

The couple at my table were dairy farmers from England who lost their herd to 'foot and mouth' disease. They were compensated and started over. They walked me home that night. It was dark enough for the city lights to be awesome, reflecting in the Salzach River, the fortress lording it over everything below.

I now understand kraut. In order to use the cabbage during the winter, they learned how to ferment it. They salted meat and fish, pickled beets, cucumbers.

I did a city tour. We went up the funicular to the castle. We went to Mondsee where Maria and Captain Von Trapp were married in the movie. The Nonberg Abbey where they actually married was too small for filming.

I then took a train back to Germany. Destination Rothenberg. I had to change trains in Treuchtlingen. It was not easy. Six minutes to go down steps from track 4, then under the tracks, and back up steps to track 7, suitcase heavy and bag on my back. Friends on the train could not help me. They had bikes. Over to side of the steps was a little moving trough where you can put the wheels of your bike. That helps move the bike along. We huffed and puffed and got on the train to Steinach with hardly a minute to spare. At that station another run, down the steps, under tracks, and back up. Train to Rothenberg.

I checked into the hotel and walked to the Old Town. Oh my gosh! The stone walls, big stone towers, half-timbered houses, cobble stone streets cutting off at angles. It was a medieval fairy tale.
On my walk I saw many pretty window treatments- white lacy curtains, window boxes of red geraniums. A guide at St Jacob's church told me all the churches were once Catholic. They were always beautiful because the people were told to give money to secure their place in heaven. After the Protestant Reformation, the churches here in Rothenberg were Protestant because the town became Protestant in 1544, shortly after Luther nailed up his 99 theses in 1517.

In the Middle Ages, people had to attend church. If they did not or went to sleep in church, a rosary was placed around their neck and they were put in the stocks. The people were told they could buy an indulgence, and their loved ones would be prayed out of Purgatory. They could not read the Bible and did not know any better. They were manipulated and deceived. That is what drove Luther to protest. The mercenary practices of the church were dangerous to the souls of the people depending on the clerics who misled them. Real salvation was hid from them.

I walked to the Christmas store. It was so big I got lost and had to ask the way out. I have always wanted to do Christmas in Germany where Christmas traditions originated. My Germany/Austria trip was extraordinary.

I continued to teach in Jacksonville, Florida, and always loved the classroom. I loved teaching writing skills, literature appreciation. I loved the interchange of ideas, the personal interaction, bouncing ideas off one another. Everything about the classroom is fun. I planned never to retire.

Carribbean, Ridgecrest, La Sabranenque, New England

2003-2006

In 2003, I drove to my brother's in Georgia. David and Vicki and I toured the Andersonville National Historic Site. In 1864, during the Civil War this Confederate prison was established to provide relief for large numbers of Union prisoners around Richmond, Virginia. Nearly 13,000 of the 45,000 prisoners died there. Clara Barton worked to have the graves marked. I found the site and the stories very disturbing.

On Sunday we drove to Plains, Georgia, attended church with Jimmy Carter and Rosalynn and had our photos taken after church with them on the lawn. I visited Kim and Blake Fielder that summer.

A Carribbean cruise sort of ushered in my year in 2004. I went with Friendship Force friends. We went to Nassau, Bahamas, the Virgin Islands, St Thomas and St Martin with the Carnival Cruise Lines. Personally I would have liked to have had more time in port and less time on the ship. The islands are beautiful. Wish we could have had more time with the inhabitants.

Our cruise director was a hoot. He told strange problems people have. One lady called the desk and said," I can't get out of my room.

I'm in my room and I can't get out!" He asked her to explain. She said," There's two doors. One is the bathroom and the other says, "Do not disturb! I don't know what to do!"

That spring break I flew to Chuck's in Jersey. We drove over to Valley Forge. Snow on the ground was reminiscent of Washington's men that winter of 1777-78 in Valley Forge. That was pretty neat.

That summer I went with my brother, Jim, and Maxine to Phoenix, Arizona, visiting Missy and her family. We drove all over the state. We walked the rim of the Grand Canyon. We drove to Flagstaff, and then Route 89A just suddenly dropped into Oak Creek Canyon. More than awesome. The road curved and dropped, curved and dropped, flanked by steep walls, and then you come out right into Sedona's red buttes and mesas. We saw Tucson, the Saguaro National Park. The OK Corral in Tombstone , Wyatt Earp, and The Walk Down shootout! Arizona is not all desert. There are some very different landscapes.

Well, sometimes, living in Florida, you just want to see the mountains. The summer of 2005, I contacted what used to be called Ridgecrest, a Baptist campground in North Carolina, when I went there in high school. It is now Lifeway Conference Center. I asked if they had a volunteer program. My idea was to enjoy the mountains, have a change of scenery from the flat Florida landscape. The answer is," Yes, we do have volunteers and many are from Florida."

I drove up for three weeks in July. I worked in the Starbucks coffee shop. On my off time I drove to interesting places every day. The first place I went was to Cherokee, to the Oconaluftee Indian village at the edge of the Great Smokey Mountains National Park. I turned onto Tsali Blvd to get to the village. I had read in my school textbook about Tsali who gave his life to save some Indians who were hiding from the Trail of Tears march. I listened to an elderly Cherokee lecture. He was so interesting I listened to him twice and took notes. Sequoyah wrote their language. The speaker said language is spiritual. If you lose your language, you lose your identity.

The Cherokee were farmers, not warriors. I believe the Cherokee were in touch with the earth and with their Creator.

I went to The Cove, the Billy Graham Training Center. Such beautiful wooded property. I went to Hendersonville, Carl Sandburg's home. Went to Black Mountain. Saw that Shaw's drama, "Arms and the Man", would be presented at a theater in Mars Hill. I had taught that play in school before. The presentation was excellent. I went to Chimney Rock, the Blue Ridge Parkway, drove to the top of Mt. Mitchell with a friend.

I saw LAVENDER on a sign in a yard. That is my maiden name. I stopped and met the man and his wife. They were gracious and let me write down genealogy from their family records. A lot of the first names were the same in our families. I never did follow through on that to know if there were any close family connections. I do know our family ancestors are English and Scots-Irish. James Webb's Born Fighting is an excellent read explaining how the Scots-Irish shaped America.

I went to Montreat to the Presbyterian Church. The trees, stone buildings, rhododendron, create such loveliness it catches your breath. The church is stone and wood, no air conditioning, open windows. It was beautiful. Nelson Bell and Virginia came here after Communists took over China where they were medical missionaries. They were Presbyterian and Montreat is a Presbyterian enclave. Ruth Bell Graham and Billy settled here near her parents since Billy was gone so much.

Faye and Phyllis took me to the church. Phyllis was married to a minister for years. They were in Africa working with the Maasai. Brother Cummins was the first to bring the gospel to the Maasai. He taught and planted churches starting in the mid 1970's until his death.

It seems my personal story is becoming one trip after another, and in 2006 there are two trips as awesome as England, Germany, and

Austria. So, I hope you enjoy two more divine appointment adventures. The summer of 2006 I worked in the Provence region of France with La Sabranenque Restoration Projects. I had met some people who did that and when I saw their photos, I knew I had to go. A French gentleman, Henri Gignoux, is the director of the association in France. The goal is to restore and rebuild historic sites, also to revitalize the traditional building techniques used in working with stone. In Saint Victor la Coste near Avignon, the group first restored an entire village. The village is on the side of a mountain. This is where we lived in neat stone cottages for the two weeks we worked on the current project.

I flew by myself, but when I got there, three ladies, Silvana Kenney, Marianne Lindquist, and Mary Fordham had arrived, along with a group of young people. The four of us ladies roomed together and became fast friends. After breakfast every morning, we were bused to the work site. But you had to walk up a mountain to get to the area where we were to build a road from stone, in keeping with the architectural style of the medieval ruins of the nearby castle, the Chateau de Gicon.

Gignoux is a perfectionist. He would speak of the stones. He said there is a marriage of the stones, the way they are placed together. He is so full of love for the intricacy of the work and wants to share his knowledge with others. We would work in the morning and eat a beautiful lunch prepared by Patrick, a professional cook, and then have the afternoon off, and again a delightful evening meal. The food was a work of art as well as the dining experience. Very casual. You are served in courses. You linger over the food with relaxed conversation. We ate outside on picnic tables. Everyone helped with the dishes.

It is hard to capture this area with a camera or with words. You need to be in the space. The little paths of stone go off at angles, the stone houses, stone walls, create an enchantment is the best I can come up with. Cicadas keeping up their songs in the trees. I would look around and could not believe any place could be this beautiful, any direction I looked.

The vegetables and fruits were grown nearby and so tasty. One meal Patrick made was chard, baked in a cream sauce, another dish of tender fresh green beans in a large platter with sliced tomatoes and onion arranged around the edge and in a row across the top of the beans. One dessert he made was small delicious melons, seeds removed, a scoop of rich Vanilla icecream dolloped inside just before serving, with the lid of the melon put back on! So creative.

Once, we took a van to Avignon and toured the Palace of the Popes. On Bastille Day we went to the Pont du Gard aqueduct, a surviving Roman ruin. Julius Caesar conquered Gaul in 59 BC. The aqueduct was built in 50 BC. We went to a museum with pictures showing the slaves carrying large stones and probably being whipped as well. I compared us picking up some rather large stones in our work, but no comparison.

The day we all left, we stood around crying. All of us, even the teenagers. We just stood around hugging and crying. What an experience those two weeks was, such a spirit of community in such a romantic setting.

I visited my friend, Louise Daniels. We were sunbathing at Neptune Beach. I told her about my trip to France and asked her if she would like us to go to New England together. I had never been. So we put together a trip in October. I took off school a week. Our plan was to see the foliage, New England authors' homes, and as we planned the trip, we joined Educator's Bed and Breakfast and arranged to stay in teachers' homes instead of hotels. It turned out totally awesome.

We flew into Boston, got a rental car and did Salem. The first stop was The House of Seven Gables, the second was Hawthorne's house where he was born. The Salem Witch Museum. The Peabody Essex Museum where we saw a very interesting Chinese house that was dismantled in China and brought to the museum and reassembled. We drove to Derry, New Hampshire, and toured Robert Frost's home. I walked in and called out, "Robert Frost, I am here!" This was an epiphany for me. I totally fell in love with his poetry in college. I loved seeing his home which is attached to the barn so that he could attend to the animals without going outside. Inside was a Singer sewing machine like my grandmother's, a wash tub and rub board, metal bedsteads like hers.

We went to Stowe, Vermont, and ate a meal at the Trapp Family Lodge. I so know about that family, how they became a professional singing group and toured for years. Wonderful story- the Captain's story, Maria's and the children, in Austria and in Vermont. I have a really nice picture book of the family I've read over and over. In Bennington, VT, we saw a lovely Congregational Church with family pews enclosed in private spaces with individual doors. Interesting. Also, Robert Frost's grave is there. Congregationalists grew out of the Puritan beliefs and practices.

We toured Alcott House which is the home of Louisa May Alcott's father, mother and the four girls. Bronson Alcott's house was the gathering place for some of the contemporary thinkers and writers of the day, 1850'-1870's. Men like Oliver Wendell Holmes, James Russell Lowell, John Greenleaf Whittier, Ralph Waldo Emerson, Nathaniel Hawthorne, Henry Wadsworth Longfellow, Franklin Sanborn. I was in hog heaven making connections with names I knew.

May Alcott, the oldest daughter, was Daniel Chester French's first sculpting teacher. He sculpted the Lincoln statue in the Lincoln Memorial as well as the Minute Man statue at the Old North Bridge in Concord.

Franklin Sanborn rescued Annie Sullivan (Helen Keller's teacher) from the Tewkesbury Almshouse. He found out she had asked to be taught to read. Then she went on to teach Helen Keller.

Mrs. Alcott's great great grandfather was Samuel Sewell, hanging judge in Salem, who later apologized. I think the whole witch thing got out of hand and people over-reacted.

Louisa May Alcott wrote <u>Little Women</u>. In the book the father goes to war. In reality, it was Louisa who went.

We went to the Old North Bridge mentioned in Emerson's "Concord Hymn", in reference to the beginning of the Revolutionary War-

> "By the rude bridge that arched the flood,
> Their flag to April's breeze unfurled.
> Here once the embattled farmers stood,
> And fired the shot heard round the world."

We drove to Boston and did the Freedom Trail and Paul Revere's house. Old North Church where the lanterns were hung to warn how the British were coming.

I loved touring Longfellow's house. Mrs. Musslewhite, my junior high English teacher, read <u>Evangeline</u> to us, the harrowing story of the Acadians expelled from their country in 1755-1764, during the French and Indian War (the North American theatre of the Seven Years' War in Europe). The expulsion was part of the British military campaign against New France.

Upstairs on the wall by the bed is Longfellow's wife's picture. The tour guide started quoting the poem, "Cross of Snow". I choked up as I began quoting with him. I knew the sonnet which is a tribute to his wife, beautifully written and sad. He also quoted a poem I had to memorize in college. These authors that I have loved- I cannot say what it meant seeing their homes and connecting with the literature I have loved for so many years.

We went to the Harvard campus. We went to John F. Kennedy's Presidential Library and Museum. I enjoyed clips of writings of Rose Kennedy written to her son.

The foliage wasn't vibrant, but it was pretty. The literary stops were great. And the teachers who hosted us were just so much fun. This was a perfect trip.

Louise and I realized we had done an over-the-top trip. We decided to try again spring break of 2007- this time the state of Virginia.

Virginia, retirement, Israel

2007-2008

Louise and I did a comprehensive tour of Virginia in March of 2007. We flew to D.C. and got a rental car. A winter storm had descended. It was cold as flugens and raining. We drove on the George Washington Memorial Parkway, eight miles to Alexandria and eight miles to Mt. Vernon, the Potomac on our left. The plantation house is situated on the banks of the Potomac. After walking and waiting in rain and cold, the tour of Mt. Vernon went in and we saw the large green dining room first, ornate ceiling and molding. On display is a large key, a gift from Lafayette, the key to the French prison, the Bastille. After the house, on to the Museum with life-size statues of Washington in different stages of his life.

We had reservations at the Mt. Vernon Inn, where we sat by a fireplace with a good fire, warm and toasty. Hot apple cider, a delicious peanut soup, corn cakes. Our adventure continued. To the car in the dark, rain and sleet build up on the glass. We headed out to I-95 S. and called our Educator's Bed and Breakfast host. No answer. We finally found the house. A woman was on the porch. She said she was our secondary hostess. She was African, dressed in a long skirt and headdress, and spoke broken English. Our host was out campaigning and we were to follow her to her house and he would be there around 10:00. We followed her for a long time, maybe 15 minutes. It was dark. It was sleeting, a bit of snow. We freaked out. Imagining everything and not comfortable, we thought we had been missput and were scared. We let her go on, took a side road, turned around and went to Fredericksburg and a Quality Inn.

Thirty-four degrees and St. Patrick's Day. We stopped at the James Monroe Museum and I did enjoy that. Monroe was minister to France during the French Revolution (1789-1799). Both Lafayette and his wife were in prison. Mrs. Monroe was able to get his wife out. He was released later. Monroe was again minister to France under Jefferson and was sent to negotiate the Louisiana Purchase. We went to the Apothecary shop. There was information on Hugh Mercer, a doctor during the revolution. He was a soldier with Washington when they crossed the Delaware at Trenton. He is in the video I bought at Valley Forge.

We drove on to Jim and Kathy May's house. I taught Kathy Allison at Strider in Mississippi. She came to Jacksonville and married Jim. Jim was now the rector of a very old historical church in King George, VA, St. Pauls Episcopal. We spent the night with them and attended the service and drove to Stratford Hall, a stately house occupied by five generations of the Lee family.

In Williamsburg, the Visitors Center, and an excellent film, the Story of a Patriot. We walked to the House of Burgesses, walked the Duke of Gloucester Street to William and Mary College and then the King's Arms for delicious prime rib with popover, asparagus, and apple cider.

We drove to Geraldine's house, our next hostess. Beautiful house, classical music, stories of her family, immigrants from Holland, nice fire in fireplace and glass of wine. The next morning we were serenaded with her playing classical music. She is a music educator and judge for the National Guild of Piano Teachers.

The breakfast table was lovely, a sausage quiche, cheese biscuits, jams, hot cross buns, fresh fruit, coffee. Afterwards, we were back in Williamsburg, enjoying mock court sessions, taking our picture in the stocks! Then to Jamestown, stopping by President's Park on the way. This was a nice surprise. There are extremely large busts of all the presidents placed on walkways at different angles and turns. A unique outdoor museum of the presidents. It is so extraordinary. And thank goodness it was warmer and a pretty day.

We drove to Jamestown. The Jamestown settlement was in 1607. Unlike the Pilgrims who came on the Mayflower seeking religious freedom in 1620, the Jamestown contingent was here to turn a profit. The Virginia Company of London financed the voyage. The expedition was all men and boys and they were soldiers and knew how to fight. After economic ventures that failed, John Rolfe, who married Pocahontas, grew tobacco and that became the money crop. Starving times, but food and more settlers came from England. The settlement survived. We visited in 2007, 400 years since 1607. We stopped by a glassblowing site, glass made from sand, oyster shell, wood ash. Saw the original church, statues of Pocahontas and John Smith.

We went to Yorktown where the American and French forces defeated the British in the last battle of the Revolutionary War. Enjoyed a lobster bisque.

On to Richmond. The St. John's Church tour was excellent. The second Virginia Convention met there. This was the meeting in which Patrick Henry addressed the group with the famous words, "Give me liberty or give me death." Previous to this, the Virginia governor had met with the burgesses and made them aware of the burden of new taxes. The patriots were unhappy and went to Raleigh Tavern to discuss the situation. King George III put so many taxes on them because he needed to pay for the Seven Years War England had fought with France (in this country the French and Indian War). The patriots would have to pay the taxes but had no representation in the making of the laws. So they had to get a plan and fight for their rights. They met at St John's Church.

Richmond is the site of Revolutionary War and Civil War history. We next toured a hospital used in the Civil War. Then the Hollywood Cemetery where Jefferson Davis, Monroe, Pickett, President Tyler are buried. We ate at Europa's. Had smoked corn and chorizo chowder, a salad with mixed greens, crispy chorizo, manchego cheese, piquillo peppers, mustard sherry vinaigrette. Yum.

The White House of the Confederacy where Jefferson Davis and his family lived during the Civil War was a very interesting tour. When Lee sent Davis word to leave because the Yankee soldiers were moving in, he took his time leaving. Lincoln came to the house after he left. Appomattox followed a few days after, Lincoln shot a few days after that. Jefferson Davis captured in Georgia a few days after that. He was still planning to find a new capital for the Confederacy and continue the fight, even after Lee surrendered to Grant!

We then drove to Montpelier. [Now, reader, we have flipped back to the Revolutionary Period.] We were too late for the tour. I know a lot about Dolly Madison and was disappointed. We drove to Charlottesville. The drive to Monticello was pretty. We were told the Virginia tidewater was the area from the Atlantic to Richmond. From Richmond to Charlottesville is the Piedmont. To the West the Blue Ridge and Shenandoah.

In the tour of Monticello, we were told the James Madisons would visit Jefferson but it would take a whole day. Also, that Jefferson would tear down and rebuild Monticello. He did not like the architecture in Williamsburg. He preferred the Greek classical style. He was a farmer like Washington, loved books, was in debt when he died; he bought a lot of things in Europe. I walked down to the gravesite. The epitaph reads, "Author of Declaration of Independence, author of statute for religious freedom in Virginia, founder of the University of Virginia."

We went on to Ashlawn, Monroe's property adjacent to Jefferson's. The picture of Washington crossing the Delaware was on a wall. Monroe was with him in the boat. We ate at Michie Tavern. It was a buffet and we piled the metal plates high with fried chicken, biscuits, gravy, mashed potatoes, coleslaw, green beans, blackeyed peas, stewed tomatoes, with tea in metal cups as well.

We went to the University of Virginia, toured the rotunda, patterned after the Parthenon. A pretty day. Students relaxing on campus in the sun. We didn't see everything in one week in Virginia, as you know, but we saw a lot.

On April 11, two weeks later, my DROP period (deferred retirement option plan) matured, and I retired from teaching at the end of the school year.

I was pretty much lost and put some things in place to keep busy. I volunteered as usher for the Wilson Center for the Arts on the Florida State College South Campus. I took some classes in square dancing. I substituted all over the school district. I applied for the Peace Corps! Then backed out. I was like, "Stop the world and let me off!" Very lost.

We had our 50th year high school class reunion in 2007. I didn't go. I have missed family reunions also. Charles Dewey Raney and I are the oldest left in our family now. It seems strange.

After Louise and I became members of Educator's Bed and Breakfast, I fixed up my extra bedroom very pretty and hosted over the years a couple from Toronto, Spokane, San Jose, also lesser known places in New Jersey, Missouri, Texas, the redwoods area of California, and D.C.

I hosted Virginia and Chuck Seal with Educator's Bed and Breakfast right after I retired. They had a friend who retired from Panama City and lived in Hilo, Hawaii. I called him to ask if he would help me apply and teach in the private school there where he taught some. We talked about me coming out there, but it was a year later before that came together.

A friend told me about the International Learning Center run by Kim Carr. She offers classes in English to people from other countries. They are also welcome to attend meetings that offer how to come to faith. I volunteered to teach in the program and Kim accepted me. I interested my friend, Trish Gillispie into teaching there also. What a fun experience. I had eight ladies: Cecilia from Peru; Carmenza from Columbia; Ayse from Turkey; Esma from Belgium; Viollanda and Flora from Albania; Marta from Honduras; Afsaneh from Iran. How I loved those ladies and they me. How I loved learning things about their country and culture. We had tea in the most beautiful tea service, good teaching materials and the cutest miniature furniture for the language lab. That was such a special opportunity for me. I dearly loved it.

For five years, I had known about Marv Rosenthal's organization, Zion's Hope, and received the magazine <u>Zion's Fire</u>. Marv is Jewish but converted to the Christian faith, a completed Jew. He has an established ministry in the Holy Land and in Florida called Zion's Hope. I saw his tour of Israel advertised in the magazine. I decided to go.

In March of 2008, the plane was late getting to Atlanta, and the flight to Tel Aviv was overbooked. Amelia, Sandra, and I were bumped and spent the night in Atlanta. I did not know them, but we became fast friends. We were one day late getting to Tel Aviv. The group had seen Tel Aviv and Jaffa, so we were shuttled to Caesarea, where we met up with the group, and I met my pre-arranged roommate, Shanti Chacko, a nice girl from India who lives in the States.

It was the first time I saw the beautiful blue Mediterranean. Caesarea was built by Herod, a Roman client King of Judea, and named after Augustus Caesar. Mike Ufferman welcomed us and told us that Herod was descended from Esau. He was an Edomite, part Jewish, but not in the line of the kings. Esau was Jacob's brother. It was Jacob who was the father of the 12 tribes of Israel and the kings of Israel. Judah is one of Jacob's sons. His line goes down to David and Solomon, the kings of Israel, and to Jesus. So the bottom line is- this bothered Herod. He was not the legitimate king. He was paranoid of losing his rule. (Remember when he had the young boys killed when he heard of Jesus' birth? The wisemen asked," Where is he who is born King of the Jews? " Herod had the babies killed to secure his throne.)

The Jews knew he was not of Jacob's line. They hated him, but he played up to the Romans and they appointed him governor and later King of Judea. Even so, Herod was an accomplished builder, not only of Caesarea Maritima, but Masada. He probably expanded the second temple in Jerusalem to please the Jews but they hated him anyway.

We drove to Cana, Nazareth, Megiddo, Mount Carmel, and went to a precipice overlooking the Jezreel Valley. While we were seated there, Marv told about Jesus reading from Isaiah in the synagogue. "The spirit of the Lord is upon me, because he hath anointed me to preach the gospel to the poor… to heal the brokenhearted, to preach deliverance to the captives… to set at liberty them that are bruised." And then Jesus said, "This day is this scripture fulfilled in your ears." They that heard him were angry because he claimed to be this savior. They led him to the brow of this hill to kill him, but he escaped. He never returned to Nazareth.

We did a boat ride on the Sea of Galilee. There was the American flag and the Star of David flag. We pledged to our flag and sang the national anthem. We pledged to the Star of David and heard their national anthem. We sang, "Fishers of Men". We watched a man throw out a huge net the way the fishermen do. Hebrew music playing . It was neat.

We drove to Capernaum where Jesus mostly lived after Nazareth. Saw the synagogue probably built over the ruins of the one he taught in. After the temple was destroyed, the people used synagogues but just for teaching. Only the temple had blood sacrifice. We stopped at Caesarea Philippi where Peter gave his confession of Jesus. "You are the Christ, the son of the living God." Jesus said that God revealed that to Peter. This is near the border of Lebanon. Went to the place where Jesus gave his Sermon on the Mount.

One day started out with baptizing in the Jordan River. I did not know you had to set that up ahead of time so I missed being baptized. Someone had asked me to bring back some water from the Jordan. I did. At home I bought some pretty little bottles for each of my four children also. I filled them and tied them with a ribbon. Once I was flying to visit my children, and the airport security stopped me and took the bottles. I tried to explain the water was from the Jordan River. She said to wait. I heard her say to her supervisor, "This lady says she has holy water…"with a kind of not-sure-what-to-do tone of voice. They let me keep the water.

We drove south, passing areas being irrigated to raise produce. We arrived in Beit Shean. Saul and his sons' bodies were displayed here after they were killed in a battle with the Philistines on Mount Gilboa.

We drove to the Qumran Caves. In 1947 a Bedouin shepherd boy threw a rock, and it hit something that broke. He went in and found what is known as the Dead Sea scrolls, ancient scrolls in containers, written by the Essenes. The shepherd boy gave the scrolls to a merchant in Bethlehem. They were sold in NY but bought by Israel and returned. They have been compared to ancient manuscripts and found identical. The Essenes, authors of the scrolls, were a disgruntled group, unhappy with the corruption in the Temple, etc: They broke off from others and built this community to prepare themselves for the end time. When the Romans invaded, the Essenes hid the scrolls in 66-69 AD., and meant to return for them, but were killed by the Romans.

Some of the group swam in the Dead Sea. I did not want to destroy my hair so I missed floating in the Dead Sea, which is fed by the Jordan River; but, having no outlet, is 30% mineral content, so you do not sink.

We departed for Masada. Masada is a mountain plateau 1400 feet above the sea level. Herod built a palace on the top in his flamboyant style. This is the story of Masada. In 66 AD., Jewish rebels fought against Roman rule and pushed the governor out of Jerusalem. Rome sent in legions to suppress the resistance. Josephus Flavius was a rebel general. He saw that the Jews could not win against Rome and turned himself in to the Romans. He became the historian for this period of time, seeing things firsthand: the destruction of Jerusalem and the temple in 70 AD.

In 66 AD., almost 1,000 rebels escaped to Masada. They grew their food. Water came from the mountains through aqueducts to their cisterns. They were self-sustaining. Roman legionnaires sought for three years to get to the top. When they finally reached the top and broke through, the Jews had killed their own families, each other and the last man fell on his sword because they did not want to become Roman slaves. Five survivors told the story. Josephus recorded it.

We went to En-Gedi where David fled from Saul, and also where Saul fell asleep and David cut off a piece of his garment, but spared his life.

Our bus headed for Jerusalem. The guide was sharing history. In 1948, the UN made Israel a nation. In 1967, the six-days war. In 1973, another war. Israel did not fare so well. Golda Meir beat herself up over that. She said she should have seen it coming. They played "Jerusalem" on the bus as we approached the city, spread out in a huge panorama, the Kidron Valley, the temple mount, the Dome of the Rock. In Jerusalem, we walked to the Western Wall, the Garden of Gethsemane. We walked the Via Dolorosa. Stations of the Cross are marked. We went to the pool of Bethesda where Jesus healed the lame man. He came there for 38 years hoping to be the first in when the angel troubled the waters. Glorious miracle, but the Pharisees were mad when he carried his bed on the Sabbath. St. Anne's Church, built by the Crusaders, not destroyed by the Muslims, was near. We went inside and sang; the music was beautiful.

It is my understanding that scribes and rabbis are working toward rebuilding the third temple, the temple of the end times, most probably. They are preparing the shewbread table, the incense altar, the menorah, the candlesticks, all the gold and brass pieces that are part of the worship in the temple. Solomon built the first temple, it was destroyed in 586 BC; Zerubbabel built the second temple after the Babylonian captivity. Herod improved on it; it is usually referred to as Herod's temple, destroyed in 70 AD.

We saw a film that resonated with me of a pilgrim coming to the temple and the preparations he made. He purchased a ½ shekel coin from the money changers, bought his lamb for sacrifice, went into the purification bath, down the steps, up the other side. It showed him approaching the beautiful, white, luminous temple. He was so in awe and ready to worship. Pilgrims attended three feasts: Passover, Pentecost, Tabernacles, during the year.

At the farewell dinner, Marv preached on hope, "Looking for that blessed hope". Hope in the scripture is sure, not speculation, not "I hope so." Our hope is in his return, our resurrection, our rapture, our reunion. We all held hands and sang "The Lord's Prayer" which culminated in raising hands, as the singing came to a crescendo in the end. We were visibly moved and tearful.

We toured the Holocaust Museum which is very well presented. It is so graphic I can't handle it. I also opted out of Schindler's Factory in Krakow, now a museum, when I was there last summer. We did see Shindler's grave in the Catholic Cemetery in Jerusalem.

A fitting ending for our Israel trip was a visit to the garden tomb and a nice communion service.

Chuck

Kaley

Karen
Zoey
David
Maddie

Jacob
Zoey
Jessica

Connie

Samuel and Synjon

Rory, Justin, Calie, Sandy, Kenny, Jennifer, Cayden, Tyler, Jessica

Rory

China and Hawaii

2008-2009

I guess these are my two Asian trips, on opposite sides of my large flat map on the wall behind my computer, but not so far apart on the globe. At the International Learning Center, I met Annette Harper, who joined a team of teachers every summer going to China to teach Chinese English teachers at a university, who were getting credit toward their certificates. I was happy to complete their team of ten.

The year was 2008. China hosted the Olympics that year in Beijing, opening August 8, thus 8/8/8. Chinese consider the number "8" a lucky number. We were located in a southern province, far from Beijing, so we could only see the opening ceremony and some of the competitions on TV, but it was an exciting time of energy and colorful spectacle. In the opening they showcased the four things China invented: the compass, paper, technology of printing, and gunpowder. The night of the opening ceremony, the local TV station came out and interviewed us and showed the clip on TV.

Our team was invited by the Chinese government to teach American culture, conversational English, and American methods of teaching English as a second language. The curriculum emphasized intonation, the rise and fall of the voice, the natural rhythm that English sentences follow with proper use of accents on syllables. Barbara coached us how to teach this. The Chinese teachers we taught were encouraged to practice their conversation skills.

Our teachers had different levels of language skills and English proficiency. We tested them in order to place them in classes according to their level. Some taught out in the villages and were not as exposed to foreigners; their English was not as good.

I want to elaborate on the word foreigner. The Chinese have a sense of national identity. They know they belong to a country with distinctive traditions and culture. They distinguish between the Chinese people and other nationalities. In an activity we did, some asked their partner, "Would you marry a foreigner?" Nelson Bell, missionary to China and Ruth Graham's father, titled his autobiography, Foreign Devil in China. The word is weighted. And the concept has hung over from a time when China was more a closed country and foreigners were feared. In the Boxer Rebellion, resented and killed. China did not recognize foreign powers as sovereign equals, but as renegade barbarians, for years.

Our teachers did like us. They would ask," Do you like China? Will you come back?"

The teachers shared their problems. They said the headmaster gets angry if classes are noisy. Their students think English is boring. Teachers have no time for anything creative, have to teach the textbook and prepare students for the test which comes from the National Board. They have 50 to 60 students in class. Their students go to sleep. They do not like English. The students have so much homework, they are very stressed.

I would hear the university students, on the campus where we were housed, orally memorizing their lessons. They would repeat, using rote memory, to learn. This is the Chinese method. In America, associative, active learning is practiced. Creative thinking is encouraged.

One of my lessons was on Chinese heroes. Of course Confucius and others. One of the heroes was Zexu Lin. He was known for his role in the first opium war, 1839-1842. He was appointed to solve the problem. He confiscated opium, blockaded trade, but the English retaliated. The British had a trade route. They bought opium in India, sold it to China, and bought tea to take back to England. It was years before this indignation to China was resolved. The class was knowledgeable of the opium wars and also happy to study their heroes.

A husband and wife couple were teachers in the International Relations Office at this university. They arranged for teams like us to come in. They oversaw our work, many meals off campus, our transportation from the provincial capital to this area, a wonderful weekend trip to an ancestral hall, Zhu's Garden, built in the Qing Dynasty, and our trip back to the capital. They worked with us on behalf of the university.

The university liked our program. We were native English speakers. Plus we were volunteers. They did not have to pay for an excellent program presented by excellent educators.

I think, in six weeks, I absorbed a lot of Chinese culture. I was so amazed while driving down the road to see corn or rice grown on every little available spot. No spot that is cultivatable is not planted.

The traffic on the road from the University to town was culture shock. You drive with your horn. People walking, bicycles, motorbikes, the vehicles with tractor fronts and truckbeds on the back, huge dump trucks, no lanes. Traffic swerves every which way. Lots of potholes. They just move over for the horn.

Foods were interesting. School cafeteria not so good. There was never any meat, just little bits. Always a big bowl of rice, green vegetables. Scrambled egg with tomato and onion. Fish soup with the head of the fish in it and the eye staring at you.

When we ate at restaurants, however, the food could be really tasty. Typical foods were: sweet and sour chicken, chicken with veggies and peanuts, pumpkin, hot and spicy shredded pork, fish, lotus. Eggplant, cabbage, cauliflower, potato fritters, bamboo or bean shoots, red and green bell peppers seasoned, goat cheese fried, tofu, rice noodles, fried bread nuggets and sweet dipping sauce. Lots of green vegetables seasoned with onion and peppers.

You always eat at a lazy Susan table, help yourself and turn the table. Once, we ate out, and Elaine Chan, my teaching assistant, ate the chicken foot and all! I never mastered the chopsticks much less a chicken foot! A teacher brought us beautiful peaches. We washed them in Clorox water to be safe.

I can't forget the squatty potties. Thank goodness, our hotel on campus had Western bathrooms, but sometimes if we went other places, there were the squatty potties. I also had to use one at a hair dressers in Turkey. I am too out of shape to do that now. You need strength in your legs to get up from the squatting position.

Of course we saw how communism played out in their lives. We were joined by a teacher while walking on the campus. Her grandmother is a believer. She would like to be but the government wants teachers to stay away from the Christian religion since they influence students. She said the government says you can choose your belief; the fact is you can't. You would lose your job.

About Tiananmen Square in 1989. A Chinese person asked our team member if anyone was killed there. The government did not tell the people the truth. Only those who were there knew. What happened in Tiananmen Square was an effort to gain democracy, but it was crushed, and then the government lied to the rest of China about the slaughter. The rest of the world knew, but the Chinese people only knew what their newspapers and TV allowed them to know.

When we had our team meetings, we closed the door and unplugged the phone in case the phone was bugged. The government makes an effort to exercise control.

On that note, I think the one child rule has been relaxed some.

We did visit one of the Three Self churches. I was glad to do that. Not an underground church, the Three Self is accepted by the government but is restricted in what they teach.

We shopped at a Miao market, one of the 55 minority groups in China. The Han people are the majority group, comprising 90% of the population. I did not know about the different groups, but I have studied Chairman Mao Zedong and his deplorable Cultural Revolution. I would hope that China today has distanced itself from that era and embraced the remnants of their ancient, rich, and colorful past with their many accomplishments.`

My friend Kevin showed me I had a movie maker on my computer. He laboriously taught me to do a photo presentation with my China photos, my Israel photos and pictures of my grandsons. Then you burn the DVD. I absolutely loved making those DVD's. I later made a Hawaii one by myself, Turkey, and Switzerland. Then that computer was replaced and I never had the program again.

My Hawaii trip no longer on the back burner, on December 28, 2008, I flew to Hilo, Hawaii, on the Big Island. Clint Brown met my plane. We went to the grocery for coffee and he bought me a pink plumeria lei. It is the custom to greet people with a lei. Clint lived way out in the country from Keauu, which is out from Hilo. Serious potholes in the road to his house. It rained the first week every day. His house, unfinished sheetrock. Not a place in the house or the yard that was pretty, just piles of junk. I never saw the blue sky for a week. Where was this Polynesian Paradise I came to see?

So, with the rain, we went to the Akatsuka Orchid Gardens which is inside. Beautiful orchids and anthurium.

Another day because of rain, we visited the Lyman House and Museum, built by the Lyman missionaries who came there in 1832 from New England on a whaling ship. I was thoroughly fascinated. I made these notes:

Agriculture: Sugarcane and rice were very large and flourishing crops in the 1850'-60's. However, there was a shortage of workers since war, famine, and disease had decimated the population. I have a book, And Then There Were None that tells how early-arriving whites brought to Hawaii the first venereal diseases, smallpox, measles, and epidemics that reduced the native population by 75% over a few decades. So, immigrants were brought in from China, Japan, Korea, and the Philippines to provide labor.

The Haili Church: Rev. Coan and Rev. Lyman were ministers. There was a great revival of religion in 1838. These missionaries also wrote the grammar books, spellers, helped develop language, trained people in carpentry, gardening; their wives with sewing, teaching, etc:

The monarchy: King Kamehameha who united the islands was the first king in 1810, followed by others. Queen Liliuokalani was queen in 1893 when the monarchy was overthrown by wealthy business owners from the States who were in possession of all the good land by that time. Probably people who were making money with pineapple, coffee, etc: They had pushed the natives into almost non-existence. It is sad to read about this. Probably most people do not know. It was a takeover similar to the near extermination of Native Americans.

The Hawaiian gods: Kane was the main god. Lonu-agriculture. Kanoloa-ocean. Ku-war. Pele-volcano. The word kapu means taboo. When the white man showed the Hawaiians they could do things considered taboo with no retribution from the gods, that system fell apart.

We saw on video in the museum the lava flow that destroyed the Kalapana area in 1990. It was so slow the people could watch it inching toward their house and nothing they could do. We drove out to Kalapana after that. It is so beautiful. A pull-off on the ocean side overlooks a black sand beach below. The road passes picture-postcard inlets. Just remembering that video made me hurt for those people.

We drove to the Rainbow Falls, and to the waterfront and saw the huge statue of King Kamehameha. We visited the Kamehameha School, a private school only for the Hawaiian children. The Hawaiian flag flying from the pole has eight stripes to represent the eight islands. In the corner is the Union Jack, the British flag, since Captain James Cook who discovered the islands, was British. We drove to Banyan Drive, a line of banyan trees like the ones I saw in China. We saw snow on the top of Mauna Loa. You can look up and see that if there are no clouds to block the view.

I applied to substitute at Christian Liberty High School. I realized it was not going to work full time. I got to fill in three days. The students were wonderful. The zoo was near the school, featuring a white Bengal tiger named Namaste!

We attended Clint's church, the Puna Congregational Church, the whole time I was there. The minister was excellent. Once Clive Cowell taught a study on Genesis. The study and discussion was exactly what I enjoy.

Clint loved to show me the island. We drove to Akaka Falls, with its 442 foot drop in the middle of the rain forest which boasted gingers 12 feet high, cup of gold vines sixty feet up in the trees, bamboo as big around as flag poles.

We saw an abandoned sugar mill operation. The union kept raising the wages. Finally the mill was so expensive, the business went to the Philippines. We walked to the shoreline which is not flat with sand like in Florida. On this shore the white breakers are booming on black rock cliffs; it's the blue fury of the ocean slamming against the cliffs and very different from a sand beach.

Once we were driving around near the ocean and this enormous, colorful rainbow was spanning the sky and dipping into the ocean. It had been raining. When the sun came out, we looked up and there it was.

By this time, we had a routine. I helped Clint work on finishing his house one day, and maybe the next day we went rambling. One of the carpentry jobs we did was he would cut the posts for the lanai and I would paint them. We were gradually cleaning up the house and yard. And I was getting to see beautiful scenic areas. I did the cooking. Two things were especially fun. He had a lot of nice plump figs. I made fig preserves and oh, so good with hot buttered biscuits. Someone gave us a coconut. I made an orange coconut pie. The chickens laid eggs, some of them green. We had "green eggs and ham"!

I should mention he had a water catchment system on top of the ground, a huge round area that caught rainwater, kept covered by a tarp, and piped into the house. We bathed with that water and washed dishes and cooked with it. Drinking water we bought in large glass containers.

We drove to the Volcano National Park, Kilauea's craters and calderas. Kilauea has been erupting since 1983. We spent the night at Gordon Morse's My Island Bed and Breakfast. I had looked forward to this. The grounds were covered in anthuriums, bromeliad, magnolias, hapu'u tree fern 20 feet tall. Such a table for breakfast: freshly-baked cranberry muffins, toast and homemade jellies, half a papaya. Gordon told me to squeeze a little lime on the papaya, fill it with pineapple chunks, crushed macadamia nuts, then yogurt. They were saying that the lava flow was quite a spectacle recently. Someone called it primordial. We did go one night, but you could not get close enough to see much. It was fun. We joined a large group and managed with flashlights and long poles to keep our balance on the hardened, black, sort of roped, roughshod lava we had to walk on.

Gordon's B&B accommodation was originally built by the Lyman missionary family's descendants. I read Sarah Lyman's book there which was published from her journal. She and her husband came in 1832. They had ten children. She had a hard life of ministry and child rearing. She talked about the rain and beautiful rain forests, the lava eruptions and earthquakes, the making of poi, made from the taro root, pounded into a purple paste and still a part of the diet. I did not like it.

Some of the things she mentioned in her diary, James Mitchner also wove into his book, <u>Hawaii</u>. Such as: Malama's brother, who was also her lover and husband, knocked his front teeth out when she listened to the missionaries and stopped sleeping with him. That is how they showed their grief. The missionaries taught against incest and the low life the whalers represented. The missionaries taught against the native women sleeping with the sailors.

We drove to Hapuna Beach. Coming back, it rained and again there was the loveliest rainbow streaming across the sky and sliding down the green mountain on down to the pasture with black cows dotting the green hillside. We drove to Kurtistown looking for a church Clint thought was there and ran into the pastor who showed us around, a beautiful little church with flowers planted all down the side, gardenia blossoms perfuming the air.

We drove to Pahoa. The saw mill there ripped ohia railway ties for the Transcontinental Railroad which was completed in 1869.

We went to a home school meeting in Hilo. I saw the article in the paper about the meeting. The Von Trapp children were there, (their aunt lives in Hilo). The four great grandchildren of Captain Von Trapp of Austria and Trapp Family Singers' fame. They sang songs from "The Sound of Music" movie and shared about their lives and their famous family and their lifestyle, home-schooled by their parents and getting to perform all over the world. Carole Phillips and I had seen them perform in Jacksonville. I loved seeing them again and hearing them share and sing.

Clint built strawberry beds one day. I sat on the lanai steps, ate a sweet, juicy tangerine, under a beautiful blue sky and white puffy clouds and trade winds. Paradise at last. That night we ran into town and got back after dark. I can still see that night sky, the stars were so definitive, like bright, sparkling diamonds on a cloudless black.

Clint and I flew to Honolulu and did the Punchbowl Cemetery, and the Arizona Memorial. Our hotel was near Diamond Head. We took a bus to the Polynesian Culture Center. I got an ink tattoo on my ankle that was cool. I would hold my leg up in the tub so it would not wash off! Waikiki Beach. We saw the deep-pink sprawling Royal Hawaiian hotel. My daddy stayed there during the war.

Back home we ran into someone who told us about an Irish/Scottish, four-generation family who entertain in town with the pipes and drums. He said this couple raised 11 children on a boat in Alaska, then moved to Mexico. The boys married Mexican women. We went to their performance. The name of the group is Lobo Del Mar. The family has 52 members. They eat together every day. They homeschool the children. As they arrived, all of the kids and grandkids came up to Carole and Rupert and kissed them. The program opens with daughters and daughters-in-law belly dancing, then the grandsons in kilts and regalia on the pipes and drums, then the granddaughters in tartan jumpers do the Irish step dance. What a performance and what a family.

Clint and I did one more trip. We took the Saddle Road to Kona on the other side of the island. We attended service at the Mokuaikaua Church. We toured the University of Nations, the YWAM University in Kona. Clint's home church has a library. I had checked out Loren Cunningham's book, Is That Really You, God? I couldn't put it down. It tells about his starting YWAM. I did not know the YWAM headquarters was in Kona until I read that book. So we planned to see the university on this trip.

I was wearing a tee shirt with Nice on the front that I had bought in France. We ran into a couple from Nice! After some conversing, we hung out with them that afternoon. Their daughter is a flight attendant with Air France so they travel a lot.

During all this time we totally finished painting, installed light fixtures, everything in the house. It looked nice. On March 18 Clint took me to the airport. He hated to see me go. I have him to thank for a phenomenal opportunity to enjoy Hawaii. I have photo albums with lovely colorful photos which is true for all my trips, fantastic memory books I love to look at and reminisce.

Jerry stayed at my house while I was gone and helped Connie with her boys and made friends with my wonderful neighbors, Edna Fletcher, Carrie Whitsell, Alma, Geri, Dave and Joy. Afterwards, Joyce, Steve, Jamie, Bill and Mila, John and Kayla, and Stephanie and Ethan.

Andrea Jones from Charleston, MS, and Galyna drove down to visit in July, 2009. They whetted my interest in visiting Kiev, Ukraine. Andrea lived there for many years, where she met Galyna who taught school there. Galyna is now in the States, going to school, working, and hoping to establish residence here. Andrea interested me in buying a laptop computer which was such as asset for me in my upcoming year in Turkey, probably the most awesome experience I ever had or will ever have again.

Turkey

2009

I was reading a YWAM Seamill Scotland newsletter. Brad Allbritton had posted an advertisement for a teacher to homeschool their children in Turkey. The ad began, "Would you like to live on the beautiful Mediterranean? In a village with the ruins of a 2,000 – year-old Greek settlement just behind a ridge to the back of our house?" He had my attention. I emailed Brad. I skyped with him and Janice maybe two times. We were comfortable with arrangements for me be their homeschool teacher for the school year.
I arrived in Antalya August 25. Brad, Zane, and Darby met me and we drove to Varsak, the village where they live, and met Janice, Allison, and Amber, and I began bonding with my host family for the next eight months. Brad works as a consultant, Janice, a homemaker.

I soon met some of their expat friends, Susan and Galav, Joe and Becky, Caroline and Catherine and Jasmine, Gladys. Wasting no time, Janice and I worked on the school schedule for Zane and Darby at my apartment which was only two houses down from their house. I would teach Zane and Darby in my school room. Janice and Susan would teach the four younger children in another room. We started classes August 31 and I loved it that Zane and

Darby moved so fast and were very sharp. They were sixth to seventh grade level. And oh, I loved studying and teaching ancient history in the land where it all started.

Early on, Brad helped me set up Skype on my laptop. I was able to communicate with my family back home. Economical, plus the phone is not convenient because of the seven hour time difference. Being around Brad and Janice was something I had never seen before. Brad read to the children at breakfast and at night. Janice read to them. Darby and Zane read all the time. As soon as they were free, they read. Brad and Janice poured their lives into the children. Consistently, Brad was head of the house and ruled quietly and with authority. He and Janice had a totally smooth relationship. The children were pulled aside quietly if there was a hitch. They adored both parents. What can you say? This was so incredible to me.

I am going to walk through my experiences I recorded in my journal and share as they happened.

We did a picnic along with four other families on a pebbled beach of the Mediterranean. The Reynolds family was there because Jadon and Sheldon would join our class on Wednesday and Friday afternoons. When I was introduced to Jim, he said," I guess this is the meet-the-new-teacher party?"

A Turkish family very close to Brad and Janice came over. She loves to cook. She made stuffed eggplant with hamburger, onion, garlic, tomatoes, spices. Fried the eggplant after partially slicing lengthwise. Scooped out the eggplant, added the cooked veggies and stuffed the skin, adding tomato paste and cooking covered. Served with rice and a thin yogurt soup with sliced cucumber, served cold. I enjoyed the food very much.

Another day, I snapped green beans. Janice pressure-cooked them with onion, garlic, tomatoes. She browned pasta, then boiled it and put a yogurt sauce on top. Fried kielbasa. Turkish bread. Another meal was substituting soy for hamburger, tomato sauce from fresh tomatoes. Add pasta, put in oven with cheese, a fresh spinach salad with apple, mandarin, feta cheese, red peppers, toasted almonds, and strawberry vinaigrette from strawberry jam, oil, vinegar. There are lemon trees in the yard, pomegranate, and olive. It is fun to go get a fresh lemon to squeeze on everything- salads, soups.

Gladys wanted me to eat with her at a fish farm at the Duden Waterfalls. It was her birthday and she shared her story. She was raised Lutheran. She read They Speak with Other Tongues by John and Elizabeth Sherrill. The name and phone number of Dennis Bennett, an Episcopal priest, were in the book. She went to his church in Seattle, near her home, and received the baptism. I love Bennett's book, Nine O'clock in the Morning. Father Dennis Bennett announced to his church in 1960 that he had experienced a new outpouring of God's Spirit. This upset his congregation. Afterwards he was offered St. Luke's Episcopal Church in Seattle, and they were open to his experience. There a Charismatic movement began and swept into churches across America.

I could relate to Gladys's testimony. It was in the 1960's that I was introduced to a new outpouring of God's Spirit as well. I am going to mention a few books that are a real blessing and so key to the baptism of the Holy Spirit in the authors' lives. David Wilkerson's The Cross and the Switchblade, Catherine Marshall's Something More, Ruth Ward Heflin's Glory, Randy Clark's There is More.

I enjoyed St. Paul's, the International Church in Antalya. Richard and Denise Moskos picked me up every Sunday for church. We became close friends. Jim and Renata Bultima started the church in 1996. Phil and Lynda were currently interim pastors. The membership has over 25 different countries represented.

I met Eddie Pong at St. Paul's. His story: After WWII, there was civil war in China. It was a fight between socialism and capitalism. The Communists were backed by Russia. They got their political ideas from Russia. The Nationalists were supported by America.

The Communist party under Chairman Mao took over China and forced the Nationalist party under Chiang Kai-Shek to flee to Taiwan. So the Western world forced an embargo on Communist China, making it difficult for China to develop infrastructure. Russia said they would give China steel and machinery, but China had to pay back in agriculture. China had to give Russia pork. One ton of steel required four tons of pork. China was poor and had to send all their meat to Russia. They could not continue, so Russia did not send any more steel. China had to make their own. The Chinese were told they had to prove they loved their country. So people built furnaces and everyone had to rip and bring iron from their house and melt it down for China's steel and machinery. Eddie was studying to be a medical doctor in China. He was forced to stop his studies and work with the molten iron. Professionals had to stop their jobs and become laborers. He was sent to a commune and starved on four ounces of rice a day. He was able to return to Hong Kong and finally recovered. After many trials, he got a visa to Scotland and started medical school over. He and Nancy live in Scotland but also have a house in Kaleici, considered the old town in Antalya and the location of St Paul's.

One Sunday Richard preached. His story: He sought God as a child and never found him. His brother was killed in Vietnam, and the family turned against God. Richard went into sin. He had a car wreck. He was all messed up and dying. Billy Graham was on the TV in his hospital room. Richard turned to God. He found him and was also healed as well! He and Denise were from Massachusetts. They worked locally at Rivendell, a Christian Retreat Center. The Center ministers to church workers who have so many problems they are dysfunctional and cannot serve on the field until they have help. It hosts teams of workers. The Center also helps Turks who are Christians to know how to live in their community.

For instance, Hussein and Fatma were some of the first believers here. They put Christian instead of Muslim on their citizenship card. Then they could not get a job. He taught Turkish and she cleaned houses. They could not change the religious designation on their card. Their family disowned them. This is a big thing. Turks are all into family. They pay a serious price to be believers. The Retreat Center was named Rivendell after the outpost in Middle Earth in J R R Tolkien's <u>The Lord of the Rings</u>. In the book, it was a refuge for the weary and oppressed. The local Rivendell was not far from our village.

I loved the village life where we lived. I looked out my window and saw the shepherd walking his sheep and goats up the mountainside to graze. The houses have outside steps up to flat roofs where people sometimes sleep in the hot summers. There is a row of caves in view on the mountain side. Sandy, rocky, sparse vegetation. Kind of an old-Bible-lands look.

In the village, I saw whole families on a motorcycle. The wife with head covered and arms covered even in hot weather. So uncomfortable looking. I would see men walking with their hands behind their backs fingering their prayer beads. During Ramadan, the people fasted all day for 30 days. They could eat at night. Then there was serious housecleaning and visiting family graves before Bayram, a three day holiday after Ramadan when people visited, gave out candy and served baklava and coke. Children got new clothes. Ramadan moves up ten calendar days every year so it is not always in the same season.

Some cultural things to mention. Drinking water was bought and delivered in large containers with a spout. You could flush the camode but not paper. Paper was put in the trash. Shoes were taken off at the door and the host family always had house slippers to offer you. Traffic was like in China, no lanes in the village, just swerve in and out.

As I have said, I was fascinated with the food. The Turkish mom came back over. She cut up onion, tomatoes, soaked lentils, added bulgur cooked with oil, garlic, mint, red pepper. They sent to the store for paper-thin bread, spread this out on a large round plate, then spread the bulgur mixture on top. We ate outside, at the picnic table under the grape arbor. Everyone rolled up with their fingers some of the pastry and bulger and ate with their fingers.

We were invited to eat at her house. She makes borek, a thin pastry stuffed with meat or spinach or feta cheese, rolled up and deep fried. She shared her terrible childhood. Her mother took something to stop a pregnancy but it killed her. Her father married again but they did not want the children. She was on the streets as a child, had a child, had to give up another child, and was married at 14. Her picture when young is beautiful. She still was beautiful and still had a hard life. We talked about childbirth. The doctors in Turkey talk 90% of the women into Caesarian sections. The good news is that God has visited this lady since this time and baptized her with a baptism of love she never knew was possible. It is a miracle.

Janice would make a ratatouille, a stir-fry of eggplant, zucchini, cauliflower, broccoli, red and green peppers, in oil, add garlic, Italian seasoning. Garlic-buttered bread in oven. Glass of wine. She also made very creamy soup. She cooked the ingredients, put in blender and back in pot to heat. She had a pressure cooker she used a lot to facilitate food preparation. We nearly always had a huge green salad for supper.

It was quite interesting to sometimes accompany Janice to the Pazaar. She went once a week. She had a roller buggy we filled up with bags of fruits and vegetables every week and they were gone by the next week. Very colorful open market. I also bought clothes there I still wear, even the Turkish pants.

One beautiful day in October we packed a picnic and drove up to Lyrboton Kome, the Greek settlement back behind their house. We saw ruins of houses, cisterns, and millstones. One of the neatest ruins was the olive oil pressing area. I took a photo of Allison standing there exactly like the one in Brad's book. I taught Allison Language Arts for 30 minutes every morning. All four younger children were homeschooled in the morning and went to Turkish school in the afternoon. Zane and Darby no longer went to Turkish school.

I thoroughly enjoyed teaching the history, Bible, the biographies and novels. The curriculum is Sonlight. It is very comprehensive and so interesting. I also took with me some really fun activities. We did them in the creative writing class we had in the afternoons. School was awesome.

Brad went to Jordan and taught a class on communication. He said to me, "It is not what you say but what people hear when you talk." They are not the same because people add their background knowledge to what they hear. He took Zane with him. They snorkeled in the Red Sea, swam in the Dead Sea, and camped out in the Wadi Rum desert! Where Lawrence of Arabia fought. A Bedouin gave Zane a beautiful robe and head piece.

I spent the night with Gladys. This time she shared about when she went on the Reconciliation Walk that Lynn Green initiated. I was given the video at YWAM Harpenden, England, in 1998. (Lynn Green is the director there.) On the walk, they gave the message to the Muslims, Jews, and Orthodox Christians that Christians are apologizing for the slaughter done in the name of Christ during the Crusades. They were trying to help soften the edge of the way Middle Easterners perceive Western Christianity. For 3 years a total of 2,500 Western Christians, keeping roughly in step with the first crusade nine centuries ago, retraced the trail of the crusaders from Cologne, Germany, through Turkey, Syria, and Lebanon, turning it into a repentance route, ending in Jerusalem. Many people received the apology.

I met Paul and Lea at St Paul's. They were leading a tour to the sites of the seven churches that are described in the book of Revelation. The churches are in the western part of Turkey, formerly called Asia Minor of course. While exiled on the island of Patmos, the apostle John was given messages to seven churches. I was happy to pay and join the tour.

We spent the night at Paul and Lea's. Becky, who was going with us, shared she had been to the Wadoni village where the five missionaries were killed in the 1950's by the Auca Indians in Ecuador. She met the man who killed Nate Saint. Most of the village is now Christian. The story is told in the movie, <u>The End of the Spear,</u> taken from the book <u>Through Gates of Splendor</u>. I know the story. I also heard Betty Elliot, wife of Jim Elliot, speak in a church in Jacksonville.

In the car enroute on our seven churches trip, Paul was sharing. He said the Turks told the Kurds if they would get rid of the Armenians, they could have their own country, but that didn't happen. 1.5 million Armenians were killed in the Ottoman Empire from 1915-1923.

Christians in Armenia were warned of this coming disaster which is graphically told in the book, <u>The Happiest People on Earth</u>. It is about Demos Shakarian's family, written by John and Elizabeth Sherrill. A boy prophet was delegated by the Holy Spirit in 1852 to warn the Armenians of the genocide in the future. The Shakarian family began to feel the urgency to act on this warning and left Armenia in 1905 and settled in California. The people who stayed in their village were killed in the massacre in 1915. Turkey denies their part in this.

Of interest: Mount Ararat where Noah's ark came to rest was always in Armenia, but the boundary lines were redrawn in 1921, putting the mountain in Turkey. So Noah's family started out in Armenia, after the flood, and years later Christianity began to spread in Armenia soon after Jesus' death. Armenia was the first country to establish Christianity as a state religion. Interesting.

Laodicea was the first stop on our seven churches tour and then we stopped at Pamukkale because it was in that area. The unreal landscape contains hot springs and travertines, terraces of carbonate minerals left by water flowing from cliffs overlooking the plain. The effect is white mountains and pools of water. It is very striking.

Philadelphia was the next church stop, then Sardis, Thyatira, Pergamum, Smyrna, and Ephesus. At each stop we read in the scripture the message that Christ gave to John concerning that church. Ephesus, our last stop, was a large city, second only to Athens and Jerusalem in the first century AD. It was one of the greatest seaports of the ancient world. A booklet I bought there states the worship of Artemis was replaced by the worship of Mary.

This could be because Mary and John lived out their lives in Ephesus. Remember, Jesus told John to take care of his mother. John's basilica is there and Mary's house. John was the only disciple not martyred. There are many ruins, the iconic facade of the Celsius Library, only a column left of the temple of Artemis, one of the seven wonders of the world, the stadium, ruins of the temple of Hadrian and the fountains of Trajan.

We did an interesting museum. Bust of Octavius Caesar. We were studying about him in school.

We stopped by an old caravan saray on the Silk Road. People stayed there overnight along with their camels. A rest stop on a famous trade route. In class we mentioned the Silk Road. Darby said, "Oh, we used to live on the Silk Road." Oh, please. Everything was too much fun. By now, you can tell I was loving my school, my family, living in the cradle of civilization.

Paul shared about Martin Luther. He said Rome would have destroyed Luther but needed Germany to fight off the Turks. Luther had friends in Germany. One strong supporter of Luther was Frederick, the elector of Saxony. The Holy Roman Emperor, Charles V, could not afford a quarrel with him, so he had to go easy on Luther. Our school curriculum covered a thorough study of Luther and Charles V, who, by the way, was a grandson of Ferdinand and Isabella, and Maximillian, Holy Roman Emperor of the House of Habsburg.

I have to brag on the four younger children, two belong to Galav and Susan. Two, the Allbrittons. These two couples switch out babysitting for each other so they can have date nights. Once, when all four children were at our house, I saw them playing. They were amazing. They got in a circle and said Bible verses and sang and loved initiating their own play time.

I loved it when Brad and kids made pizza. Toppings were tomato sauce, smoked sausage, red peppers, hot peppers, olives, pineapple and lots of cheese. Once, I took his picture, cutting the pizzas with scissors. It was his 43rd birthday. When we had pizza, we ate in the family room and watched a movie. No one watched TV otherwise. In some American homes the noise and the news,(that is mostly drama anymore,) is never turned off. One movie we watched was Kung-fu Panda. Some of his sayings: "You meet your destiny on the road you are taking to avoid it." "Today is a gift. That is why they call it the present."

When I came into the country, I paid $20.00 at the airport for a three month visa. That time was up. Brad drove me and Lora, a teacher homeschooling in Antioch, to Kas, in Turkey, where we caught a ferry to a Greek island, paid the money, re-entered the country, and our visas were re-instated for another three months. It was a beautiful drive in the Taurus Mountains.

Janice was asked to give the message at church. She said God could give us a spiritual shot in the arm to last a while, but, No, he wants a relationship, an ongoing conversation. He wants to be our friend. Joe preached one Sunday. His message was God could do his work apart from us, but he chooses to engage us to be his hands and feet, to partner with us.

I visited with Lynda and Phil, from Wales. We watched the movie, <u>Amazing Grace</u>, the story of William Wilberforce and his long effort to get Parliament to abolish slavery in England. John Newton had been a captain of a slave ship for years. He repented, wrote the hymn "Amazing Grace" and became a minister. Wilberforce asked him to speak to Parliament of his firsthand experience with the horrors of the slavery system. Wilberforce finally persuaded Parliament in the early 1800's to stop the slave trade in England. For Thanksgiving we all went to Rivendell and spread a huge table with all the Thanksgiving foods. I made the cornbread dressing. The weather turned cold. It was finally winter. The bad thing is if there is no sun, the water is cold since it is solar-heated. The wood heater was put up in living room, Christmas tree up. Janice and I typed up the report to send a summary of what my two students had accomplished to the Sonlight home school agency.

Christmas was a big celebration. Richard, Denise, and I went to a <u>Nutcracker</u> performance. It was wonderful, costumes, choreography, and orchestra were delightful. Our kids were in charge of a Christmas program at church. The four young ones were beautifully dressed in clothes from India. They did a song, "Where is the one who is born the King of the Jews?" The older kids did an interpretive skit of the three wisemen. Zane wore his Bedouin outfit! Here comes the incredible. On December 24, we loaded in the van and drove to Susan and Galav's and caroled them with lighted candles. They then piled in the van with us. We drove to Caroline, Catherine, and Jasmine's and caroled them. They piled in the van. We caroled Gladys. She piled in and we drove up a very steep road to carol Joe. Becky was in the States. I will never know how that van made it up that very steep grade or even how we all got in it to start with.

Christmas day the children were so excited. They got lots of gifts plus boxes from Brad's mother. I fried bacon someone 'quietly' gave them. Had a good breakfast including a huge fruit salad. Then the gifts. I got a beautiful blue scarf, an Antalya mug, Turkey carpet mouse pads, <u>The Kite Runner</u>.

The next day was Boxing Day. We celebrated at Gladys's. Food, games, white elephant gifts. I got a pair of red Santa Clause boxer shorts!

My landlord brought me a bowl of Noah's pudding. It is supposed to reflect foods that Noah had left at the end of the time on the ark. Fruits, grains, whatever they could scrounge up. It was tasty. Muslims do this at this time of the year and share with neighbors. When I worked at the International Learning Center, one of my students and her husband came and made it for us. And so the year 2009 came to an end. Happily, 2010 would bring more adventures.

Turkey and Switzerland

2010-2012

January 3- Richard and Denise and I drove to Perge, about nine miles east of Antalya. Perge was once an important city in Pamphylia, spelled Perga in the Bible. The apostle Paul journeyed to Perga as well as to Antalya, spelled Attalia in the Bible. Sizable impressive ruins of rows of columns, Roman baths, sheep cavorting over the fallen stones. There are excavations being done. Sculptures were taken to the museum in Antalya for preservation.

Janice, Ebru and her daughter and I went to the Hamam, the Turkish bath. It cannot be described. You go in a very hot room, strip down to your swimsuit bottoms. Pour very hot water over you, buckets and buckets. Then lie on a table and a lady scrubs you with a coarse glove. Piles of dirty skin roll off. Some older women walking around with their endowed sagging body parts. Hilarious.

It was time to renew my visa again. You had to leave the country and come back in. I knew that Flora, from Albania, whom I taught at the International Learning Center in Jacksonville, had family in Athens. We set it up that I would fly to Athens and visit her sister, two brothers and mother, renew my visa and re-enter Turkey. They were so gracious. They took me to the Acropolis, the Parthenon and to the Corinth Canal, a Cretan restaurant, and shopping. I bought Greek sandals. We could not communicate, but the children knew enough English to help. It was lovely to meet them.

I very much enjoyed the time Jasmine and I flew to Istanbul. She was eager to accompany me and show me the city. I love church history and I am going to digress here, and you will see why this trip was significant for me.

The church, that Jesus Christ set in order when he left, continued, even under persecution, until Constantine, a military strategist, who was converted in 312 AD, became Emperor and sole ruler of the Roman Empire and combined the church and state. The word catholic meaning universal, in time the church was known as the Roman Catholic Church.

Struggles over doctrine led to a council in 325 AD. The Nicene Creed was drawn up which settled forever the question of Christ being very God of very God, one with the Father and not created by Him. The bishop at Rome was the head of the church.

When Constantine saw Byzantium, on the Black Sea, between Greece and Turkey, he loved it, conquered it and renamed it Constantinople. He made the city the Eastern capital of the Roman world, Rome being the Western capital. Constantinople preserved Greek art, Roman law and Christianity. It was the strongest and richest city in the world for 1100 years.

Around the 400's and 500's barbaric tribes descended on Europe. The Dark Ages drew a curtain over what was once the mighty Roman Empire. Mighty Rome in the western part of the empire was decadent. Only in Constantinople, in the eastern part of the empire, of all the civilized world, was the light of learning kept brightly burning.

During this time Justinian built the Hagia Sophia in 537 AD. in Constantinople. It was a Christian church. Constantinople fell to the Turks in 1453 AD. I have a book that vividly puts you inside the character of the last Christian Emperor who anxiously watched, for days, the Ottoman Turk armies approach and lay siege to the city. Sure enough, in the attack he was killed. Constantinople fell and Christendom.

The Hagia Sophia became a mosque. Constantinople became Istanbul. I was very glad to tour the Hagia Sophia which is now a museum.

This is interesting. Out of the Byzantine libraries, 120,000 manuscripts disappeared when the city fell. Many of them turned up eventually in Italy. With the classical knowledge they spread, these stolen books became one of the foundation stones of the Renaissance.

We also toured Topkapi Palace, where the sultans lived for four centuries. We went inside the Blue Mosque. We did a cruise on the Bosphorus, the waterway that divides Istanbul; the European side is to the left and the Asian side to the right. From the boat we saw a building Florence Nightingale used as a hospital in the Crimean War.

I saw a book on Gallipoli in a book store. In WWI, the Central Powers had blocked the Dardanelles (the strait that connects the Mediterranean to the Black Sea) so the Allies could not get through to Russia (who fought with the Allies). Churchill got the idea to open that up at Gallipoli, just north of Troy. He thought the Turkish forces (fighting with Germany and the Central Powers) were not that strong. But Attaturk held that area and his leadership in the war led to his being in position to fight for and win Turkish independence after the war. The Allies at the end of the war were going to carve up Turkey, but he mustered forces and won independence for Turkey and was the founder of the Republic of Turkey. He is much revered, statues and photos of him are prevalent.

Back in Antalya, my students planned a surprise party for me. We met at the Bultemas. Their daughter Talya also attended our afternoon classes. The kids cooked the food. All their parents were there. It was a nice evening.

Dee Ann, Jadon and Sheldon's mom, does a Shakespeare Festival at the church every year. We prepared a play. She drove us into town to practice the play at the church where we would perform it.

The Allbrittons had not been to Cappadocia so we planned a trip together before I left to go home. We drove through beautiful mountains heading northeast to the Nevsehir Province. This region is known for its distinctive "fairy chimneys", tall, cone-shaped rock formations clustered in Goreme and elsewhere. Homes are carved into valley walls. They are called caves, and they are fairy tale as well. We stayed in one of the caves.

It was Easter morning. We watched the hot air balloons and then drove to an underground city. The Derinkuyu underground city is an ancient multi-level (8 levels accessible) underground city with a depth of 200 feet. It could shelter 20,000 people with livestock and food stores. Huge circular stones could close off the entrances. The cities were used in the Byzantine times as a refuge for invaders. Example, Christians escaped Arab invaders. The cities were self-sustaining, including chambers for churches, kitchens, wine and oil presses. An underground water supply. We had to bend down low to get through some of the tunnels. I don't have words for these incredible labyrinths of caverns, only discovered since 1963. The ingenuity is incredible and besides they are amazing.

We did a three mile hike in an awesome countryside. We visited a carpet factory and watched the girls weave the rugs, and the salesmen throw the carpets out on the floor with a spinning motion to interest us in buying. Janice and I went to a dinner theater and folk dance floor show. We bought our tickets from Mehmet who owns the Fred Flintstone Bar and a tourism company. He was born in a "cave" near ours. He started the first hotel in Goreme in 1984. Tourism started in Cappadocia in 1984. He said this area was the center of the Hittite civilization which we studied in our curriculum. They were known for their horses and pottery. On the way home we stopped in Konya which is the Muslim name for Iconium in the Bible. The whirling dervishes have a Sufi Order in Konya. They practice the art of meditation as they whirl. Jasmine and I saw a dervish at a restaurant in Istanbul.

Well, I did it all. The Turkish bath, ate delicious Turkish food with the local families sometimes sitting on the floor, smoked the nargale pipe, had raki (a black licorice drink), watched the whirling dervish do a dizzying performance. Lived in the village with the women covered and the sheep and goats grazing outside my fence. Walked where some of the apostles walked, thoroughly enjoyed my host family and all their friends. Taught amazing kids creative writing and ancient history not so far from the Mesopotamia Valley where civilization started, not so far from Mt Ararat where the ark landed, and right in the middle of where the gospel message first spread out to the rest of the world.

Saturday we had the Shakespeare Festival at the church. Fifteen church children either played an instrument or recited a poem. My students did our play "The Happy Journey" by Thornton Wilder. I sat for a photo with my students. Jim took it, left, and came back with the photo on the cover of a little booklet they had prepared for me. Each student had written me a note. I have it on my piano. Sunday, April 11. My 71st birthday. Brad drove me to the airport.

Back home. Later that summer, when I realized that YWAM was celebrating 50 years since its founding, and Loren Cunningham was visiting a lot of the bases, I determined to volunteer at the base in Lausanne, Switzerland, where he first started the Youth with a Mission organization. That was his first base. I had never been to Switzerland so I contacted the YWAM base. Louise decided to join me and there you go. We were officially Mission Builders.

We flew to Geneva and took a train to Lausanne where they picked us up. The staff was friendly and helpful. Our first work assignment was laundry. A lot of DTS (Discipleship Training School) students had just been there and left tons of bedding to be washed, sheets and duvets. We still talk about how we had that job down. We had a system. When that was caught up, we worked in hospitality some. Helped cut up veggies for the morning break and washed up, some light housekeeping.

Geeta, who travels with the Cunninghams, helped me set up Skype on my laptop. She shared her unique testimony. When Jesus appeared to her personally in a dream, she became a believer. I have heard of this more than one time. I heard testimonies like this in Turkey.

Louise and I worked in the morning, ran off rambling in the afternoons and came back for supper. The food was really good. Our accommodations were a nice bedroom with single beds and private bath. Nothing short shrift at this base. Everything was pleasing and convenient.

The bus stop was in front of the base. We would take the bus to the metro and go the end of the line and get off at Ouchy, on Lake Geneva. One day we did that and went to the Olympic Museum, or we would get off the metro at the Gare stop and take the train on the weekends daytripping.

One weekend we went to Vevey, Montreux, and the Castle of Chillon made famous by Byron's poem. To Gruyere where we watched a cheese-making process. One weekend we took the train to Berner Oberland through Interlaken and on to Wengen. Checked into our hotel, Edelweiss, and took a cogwheel train on up to Kleine Scheidegg. I believe the Alps were the most beautiful scenery I have seen anywhere. I think I would have to say that.

We went to Bern and walked around. Went to Lutry and took a little tourist train, the Lavaux Express, up in the vineyards. One weekend we went to Geneva to the church where Calvin preached during the Protestant Reformation. Saw the United Nations building but it was closed. Toured the Red Cross Museum. We took a boat to Evian and to Yvoire, both on the French side of Lake Geneva or Lake Leman. Yvoire is totally medieval with the walled city, greenery and flowers, and tourists! Medieval cities always take my breath away. Avignon in France, Rothenburg in Germany, now Yvoire. That time period is just romantic, isn't it? I guess we think of castles and knights and Camelot--

Louise I wanted to experience fondue. Astra made fondue for us and asked a few friends for a small social.

I meant to stay until Loren Cunningham arrived but my knee became intolerable and we flew home after a month. I had to have arthroscopic surgery, but that trip was right up there with the rest of them.

When I got home, my grandson Samuel was in the fifth grade at Seacoast Academy, a private Christian school. He had had a slow start in grade school. I decided to pick him up every afternoon and tutor him. He advanced by leaps and bounds. He worked hard, and I dearly loved working with him. This continued in his sixth grade year at Seacoast Middle School. I really enjoyed his English, history, and Bible courses.

Then both my grandsons went to live with their dad, and I was wanting something to do.

Turkey

2012-2013

I wanted to go back to Turkey. Zane and Darby were 11th grade now. The family wanted me back. They were in the States, so we connected in New York and flew to Antalya together. This time they rented an apartment across the street and I would have a roommate. The school would be a co-op with four families represented. Classes would meet in our apartment on the bottom floor of the neighbor's house.

We arrived September 1. I was happy to be back with this family. And happy to meet my roommate. Anya arrived from Ukraine. She lives about two hours' drive from Kiev. She would teach twin sisters in the Hudson family. The Mehrotra children, the Allbritton children, and the Shelton children rounded out the co-op.

I was interested in Anya's story. She studied in college how to teach ESL, English as a second language. She went to the States as an au pair. Then back to Ukraine. About Soviet countries--Anya shared that under Communist rule people were sent to Siberia. The government lied and said they were evil dissidents, so their families who were left were treated badly and could not get jobs. A person's neighbor might not like him and turn him in. He could be deported with no questions asked. Soviet countries got independence from the USSR in 1991. For the first time people could go to church. Many denominations came in to make the gospel available. Her family is Pentecostal.

Janice went in with me to church until I could get used to the buses. The family that picked me up three years ago for church was no longer there. I would have to ride the bus from the village to the city to church. On the bus we met several families going to church who are teachers in the Gulen schools.

I was happy to start school. The history this year was not ancient history but 20th Century history. Our first reader was so high interest for me, God Spoke Tibetan. What an impossible story of how God got the gospel message to the Tibetans. I do not know where the researchers for the Sonlight curriculum find such remarkable books.

Well, this is fun and makes what I just said on point. I went over to have breakfast with my family. They had guests who had spent the night, Magnus and Maria, from Sweden, who now live and work in Turkey. We ate outside. I got a nice photo of them. Magnus and Maria were church planters in Mongolia and worked with Brian and Louise Hogan there. Brian wrote a book, There's a Sheep in my Bathtub about their experience there. That book was the final reader in our curriculum, another excellent choice. But my story doesn't end there. Back in Jacksonville, I went to hear Brian Hogan speak and took his picture with my two grandsons, Samuel and Synjon. So I personally met the two families who worked in Mongolia, with significant success.

Our landlords were eating outside and asked us to eat. Brad was in conversation with the Turks about people in the States picking up fast foods from drive-thru's and maybe eating in the car. The Turks said, "There's no food culture in America?" In the village, families often eat in the yard. It is family time while enjoying food and interaction.

Anya said when she was in America, she met a family, Amir and his wife and daughter at the Vineyard church, and was asked to live with them two years. They now live in Dubai but came for her birthday.

Amir told us his story at the birthday party. He was raised in a very religious Muslim home in Iran. He did all the rituals when a teenager. He told his father he felt nothing. His father told him he was not supposed to feel anything, just follow the rituals. Amir did not agree with praying toward Mecca or waking up at 4:00 in the morning to pray. Finally he told his father he would just be an atheist. He did not agree with serving a god who might be in a bad mood when he got to eternity and send him to hell. He said it says that in the Koran. His father told him to go to America and live with all the unbelievers there. Then he could go to hell by himself and not disgrace the family by being a bad Muslim. Amir went to America and met Christians. He was prayed for and he said the darkness began to lift and he was able to hunger for the Word. He read the New Testament, accepted Jesus and was spirit-filled. He went to America in 1976. In 1979, Iran became an Islamic state. He did not go back to Iran.

Hasan, our landlord, had a sheep and a goat penned up for the sacrifice festival. We watched him and his son slit their throats. Every family kills an animal, cooks some and gives some away. We were invited to eat with friends, community style from the same dishes. A big family and delicious food.

The Mehrotras and the Allbrittons decided to go on a camping trip to Olympus. We drove two hours in the mountains and set up camp. I had my own pup tent. The kids loved climbing the trees and playing dodge ball. We walked up to the Eternal Flame. Methane gas seeps through vents in the rocks and causes a constant fire to burn. The kids roasted hot dogs over the flames. I slept in my clothes both nights and used a plastic cup to pee in the squatty pottie bathroom so I wouldn't have to squat.

We ate one meal inside that the camp owners cooked. It was the National Holiday commemorating when Attaturk set up the Republic. On TV they were showing a celebration and people in the streets protesting the move from secular to religious government that the Prime Minister seems to be pushing. That was in 2013. Now in 2017, Erdogan is president and is pushing for an authoritarian government.

Back to school. Zane was doing his research paper on the Great Depression in the States. I skyped my Aunt Virginia for anything she could remember during that time. We also planned to include a photo of me around five years old and my Aunt Virginia around 25 years old sitting in a swing. I had the photo with me on a thumb drive.

I found a whole collection of missionary biographies written by Janet and Geoff Benge shelved with the school books. I took them to my room, put them in order by dates and during the course of the year, in my free time, I read and did summaries. I like biography and especially following people's stories on their Christian journey.

Tim and Casey were invited for supper. We had cheeseburger soup and homemade biscuits. Tim told the amazing experience he had in Columbia, South America. He went with a missions team, and God just showed up. Tim would share with the people in English and they would understand in their language. He was ministering with his team, standing in front of the church. The people came up for prayer and the team hugged them, but God put such a love in Tim to give to them. It was a love he never felt before. He was overwhelmed. The grown Columbian boys melted. Tim was totally changed. He went home and told Casey. They both knew they wanted to quit their jobs, sell everything and go into missions.

Our neighbor ladies wanted to ride with us to the Pazaar. Debbie was with them, a British lady from Cornwall, who was dating a brother of our nextdoor neighbors. I knew Daphne du Maurier from Cornwall wrote <u>Rebecca</u>, one of my favorite books. I asked if she knew her. Debbie said when she was a child, she used to see the famous author out and about in Cornwall. More on Debbie later.

One surprise after another. The bus terminal moved just behind my house! There is no way to say what a convenience that was. I was next door to the bus terminal and a straight shot to church! I took the bus to a Christmas tea at the church and spent the night with Paul and Lea and picked out a bunch of their movies to borrow, the <u>Christy</u> series (stories of Catherine Marshall's mother who was a teacher in the Appalachian mountains) and the <u>Anne of Green Gables</u> series to watch with my host family. At church that Sunday, the pastor asked me to light the advent candle. When I got home, Aysegul, Janice's friend had brought cabbage rolls, green peppers stuffed with rice, those bulger fingers, a lemon cake. There was a fire in the wood stove. Nice.

We always finished our school classes by noon. In the afternoons we started working on SAT preparation, and I also started helping Rebekah, a beautiful Kurdish girl, prepare for the GED.

Our school work was heavy on history, a lot of wars and depressing at times. One of the many books dealing with war was <u>All Quiet on the Western Front</u> which was troubling. Excellent biography of Churchill—The students had to type a decade summary of the main players and events when we finished each ten years of 20th Century world history.

But then one of our books was <u>Kon-tiki</u>. In 1947, five guys led by Norwegian explorer, Thor Heyerdahl, set out to show you could get from Peru to the Polynesian Islands on a raft. Possibly that was how the islands were populated. I was mesmerized reading the book. Their sense of adventure and daring was unreal. I told the kids someday I would see that raft but I never in a million years dreamed I would. In 2014, Louise Daniels and I were in Norway and I went to the Kon-tiki museum and I saw the Kon-tiki raft! On the train I met a lady whose science teacher was Thor Heyerdahl's son. How fun it that? How fun is life with this family in Turkey where I always met fun people, and encountered fun knowledge, day after day.

We ate supper with the Mehrotras. She had chicken seasoned with curry in gravy. The best black beans. Green salad. Cappuccino with Baileys Irish cream! Just wow.

In the news- NATO was asked to help at the border where Syria is bombing their people. Assad is backed by Iran, Russia, and China, so 60,000 Syrians have been killed and nobody can really help them.

Again the Mehrotras and Allbrittons decided to do another excursion, this time to Fethiye. It is a port city on the coast known for its rock tombs. We came up on snow for miles on our drive through the mountains. In Fethiye we found a nice hotel overlooking a bay and mountains. We went to the ruins of a Greek town, a village called Kayakoy to see the abandoned Greek village.

I am going to set up this history again for the backdrop of what happened here. It started with Attaturk rising to fame in WWI by repulsing the Allied assault at Gallipoli in 1915-1916. He then established a national government and convened a national assembly. He inspired the nation to reject the postwar division of Turkey and defy the occupying forces. He abolished the Sultanate and deposed the Sultan.

Attaturk also fought Greece. Greece ordered 100,000 troops into Anatolia to support the Greeks in Izmir. Attaturk led his army to defeat the Greeks. Then there was a population exchange in 1923. Greeks had to leave Turkey. Turks had to leave Greece. I suppose the idea was to solidify Turkey into a nationalist state.

So here was this abandoned Greek village, the result of the population exchange. Only the stone walls of the houses remained, about 2,000 houses on the slopes, with roofs, doors, windows ripped off.

Turks coming here from Greece settled on the plains. They were farmers. They did not move into these abandoned Greek houses. It is so disturbing to imagine the heartache that is part of this whole thing. You look out over the landscape of skeleton houses, and you imagine this uprooting and sorrow. We walked in the area and then ate gozleme in the restaurant.

Ready for the next unbelievable episode? Debbie, from Cornwall, would meet me in Bristol! She had gone home to England for a short time and while she was there she suggested I could fly to London and take a bus to Bristol. She would show me around Cornwall.

Unfortunately, I was nervous on arriving at the airport and picked up the wrong bag, identical to mine, in London airport baggage claim. I had to do passport control, ATM for 300 pounds, get the bus ticket, and was nervous. Really you walk right out of the airport and the bus terminal is right there, but I was nervous.

When we checked into our B&B in Bristol, I realized I had the wrong bag. We lived a horror story with her calling every day for days to try and return that bag and get mine.

I had researched and found John Wesley's chapel in Bristol. What a delight to go there. I stood in his pulpit for a photo! We toured his living quarters upstairs. I have read so much about Wesley, his life, his training from his mother, his ministry. So special to see the oldest Methodist Church in the world. Wesley and his brother, Charles, ministered in Georgia, on St. Simons Island, just north of Jacksonville, Florida. I have been there several times.

We started our drive for Cornwall. The weather was cold and raining. Her car died on the road. We were towed to her son's house. While we were there, the airline picked up the suitcase but did not bring mine. Debbie stayed out the next day buying a car. She had bought me a book with four of du Maurier's novels in it. All day I read <u>Jamaica Inn</u>. When she came in, we left to go eat at Jamaica

Inn, not so far from us. I really wanted to get there before dark and we did and got photos. This was a pirate's den. A lot of dark things went on. Wreckers of ships, murder, smuggling. I had read this book all day. I was so hyped and then was thrust right into this atmospheric inn where the smuggling and the murders happened in real life and in the book. Too much fun. We ate by the fireplace, steak and ale pie, apple pie and clotted cream. We spent the night, had an English breakfast and were told to notice a tin mine in the area. Used to be a big business in Cornwall.

We started down the coast to Lands End, to St Ives and Mousehole. I love the dry stone fences, covered in ivy. We saw fishing villages, towns on steep hills with narrow streets built for dray horses and buggy, not a car. We stopped in Fowey at a museum with du Maurier's memorabilia. Found a carvery and enjoyed a good Yorkshire pudding.

Here you go! We took my picture on the Plymouth steps where the Mayflower set sail in 1620! It just gets better and better, doesn't it? We drove up to Plymouth Hoe where it is told that Sir Francis Drake was playing bowls while he waited for the tide to change before sailing out with the English fleet to engage with the Spanish Armada. It was freezing cold. I was wrapped up and had borrowed boots from Debbie.

Debbie took me to the bus and I left for Cardiff, Wales, to visit Phil and Lynda whom I knew the first year in Turkey. They had moved back to Wales. They met me and picked up fish and chips. Lynda took me the next day to a castle and we went to her mother's and borrowed clothes for me to go to church the next day. After church we went with friends to a carvery and had honey-baked ham, roast beef, roasted potatoes, carrots, green beans. Put that in your plate and then they poured wonderful gravy over the top of it. We went home and watched rugby on TV. England and Ireland were playing. Each team, the men lined up with arms around one another's shoulders and sang their national anthem with fierce loyalty! No pads or helmets. They piled on top of each other during the game.

Scotland, Wales, Ireland, and Cornwall are Celtic. There is a lot of rivalry between these countries and England.

What a pleasant surprise Phil had for me the next day. He took me to Moriah Chapel, Evan Roberts' church. Evan was a leading figure in the 1904-1905 Welsh Revival that spread through Wales and beyond. They were having a prayer service. We joined a handful of people and sang songs from old hymnals in this very historic church. On the way home we drove to a village with coal miners' cottages row after row.

When I left the next day, Phil gave me a book on Evan Roberts' life. It is hard to say what all of this meant to me. In London, with some trouble, I retrieved my bag, having to make do all that time. Someone had stolen my camera battery charger from my suitcase. The Reynolds now lived in Texas but would be visiting Turkey, so I got her to bring me a generic one.

Dennis Massaro who worked at Wheaton College for years is a friend of Jim Bultema, the pastor at St Paul's. Jim asked Dennis to be interim pastor while he worked on his doctorate. Dennis is an extraordinary minister. I loved hearing him on Sundays. One Sunday after church, I ate with Amanda Jordan whom I met earlier. She had taught in China for five years and we were studying China. I wanted her to come out and share with my kids.

Here comes a hic cup in the road, but it was pretty neat. On the way to church, after I took the second bus,(you had to change buses) I knew the route was wrong. I finally said to the bus driver, "Kaleici?" He motioned, "One moment". He soon stopped, opened the door, pointed, and said,"Kaleici." I did not have a clue. We were not in the area of the church. A high school boy got off with me and asked at an office when the tram left for Kaleici. Then he stayed with me and with limited English and his electronic dictionary, he managed to tell me that because of "Run Antalya", a sports activity, the road had been blocked that the bus normally took. He got on the tram with me, and in a moment, someone yelled, "Marilyn!"

It was Kristen who had been sidetracked also getting to church. I was glad to see her, but the Turkish boy had rescued me. He was amazing.

On the buses, when I got on, someone always got up and gave me a seat. They are respectful of senior citizens.

Renata asked me to sing Saturday night at the Women's conference. Someone played for me and I sang three choruses. I was so "in voice". My voice and anointing was strong. I was so psyched I couldn't go to sleep that night.

A strategic missions DTS was in progress. The ladies met at Gladys's and Becky was in charge of a fun activity. Everyone told their name and if they liked their name, then a favorite stuffed animal as a child and why, then a great experience on the mission field. This was such an ice breaker. I met Liz who has been to Cambodia. We studied the atrocities there in 1975-1979. She said the country still has an orphan mentality.

Absolutely delightful afternoon with Amanda Jordan. She came and told so much about her five years in China for us since we were studying China. She said the Three Self Church is controlled, but at the house churches and the English corner, the Chinese are taught the full gospel and are free to believe; actually she said you can just share with someone and they are ready to believe. She shared openly in her classroom and nothing happened.

Amanda says it is hard to control a large country. Many times Christians are left alone until something happens to alert the government. Then they make arrests and haul someone off to save face.

China's government is all about saving face. They pretend that there is freedom of religion but the opposite is true. My students in China said the same thing. The government made over Billy Graham and imprisoned a Chinese believer at the same time.

Amanda knew Jeff and Anya who are here in Turkey. When she left China, they suggested she come here for a while. She made good money there, taught at a university monitoring tests for people getting their ESL certification. She said there are so many people in China. I saw that in Kunming. Getting around by bus is a nightmare. It would take a full day to get to her doctor and back. You have to get the bus ticket ahead so that is another trip. Her phone was tapped. Foreigners have to be careful not to go to the house churches and gatherings of Christian Chinese. They draw too much attention.

She met a Christian who was five generations down from Hudson Taylor's ministry near Shanghai. She said that area is heavily Christian.

Mark Wilson taught at the SOFM school, for those preparing for foreign missions. He taught the apostle Paul, John, and Peter's ministry in Asia Minor. I got to go with the group the next day to Perge, Aspendos, and Side, places with Roman ruins.

I got to go with Darby to her piano lesson. Rebekah was there. After Darby's lesson I got to play and sing for the teacher, Darby, and Rebekah. The piano her teacher had bought in Istanbul. It belonged to an Ottoman Turk princess.

Wonderful church service. A conference for international pastors was held at the church all week. They were from Moscow, the Netherlands, Copenhagen, London, Zurich, Berlin, Brussels, Vienna, Paris, Bonn, Lucerne, Nova Scotia, Tokyo, Geneva, Stockholm, and Iraq. My international church that I love.

It was the day of ballet performances one morning at the school and that night at a large theater at the Sea. It was Children's Day in Turkey. Amber, Allison, Samantha, and Ned performed in dances. I loved seeing them perform.

Ben King and I were friends at church. Our school was done and I was waiting to go home. He and I did some local daytrips, to Attaturk Park for lunch overlooking the beautiful blue Mediterranean Sea, to Phaselis and to Sagalassos which are neat Roman ruins. We also saw a strip of 5-Star hotels. Like Las Vegas. That was a whole different view from what I knew of this area.

I do not know how to compare my two years in Turkey. They were different but both loaded with such interesting people and different experiences. I would love to be there right now. Life there is a page turner.

Norway, Prague, Italy and Ireland

75th Birthday

2014-2015

One of the highlights of 2014 was my 75th birthday April 11. All four of my children came. Chuck and Karen flew, Kenny drove, and Connie is here. Karen had arranged the celebration with the Alhambra Dinner Theater. We drove up, and there was my name on the marquee outside all lit up. Inside another welcome sign. During the meal they had me stand and they read out a little script that Karen had prepared about me. The performance of The Color Purple was good. I am proud of the nice photos of the five of us.

Marilyn, Karen, Chuck, Kenny, Connie

Throwback 1993 Georgia

Pastors Steve and Jackie Kuhn and my church friends came to the house for house church and potluck dinner. Pastor Steve gave a teaching and the boys played their horns. Cindy Lavender Burch drove down to see her cousins. We live too far apart to get together very often so this was an extra special occasion. I am honored they put it together.

Chuck is currently in between operations manager at the fuel farm that services Atlantic City airport and getting his commercial driver's license. Kenny owns and operates two skating rinks in Jackson and Athens, Georgia. Karen is a medical transcriptionist in Grenada, Mississippi. Connie works with pediatric home health in Jacksonville, Florida.

Chuck drives to Philadelphia and plays trumpet for a mega church. He has enjoyed calling in on a radio program and sharing scripture and his thoughts onthe topic discussed. Kenny has played trumpet in his church for years. Karen headed up the music in her church for several years. Connie headed up the children's ministry in her church for years.

Now for my bucket list trip: the Kon-tiki museum, Prague, and Italy.

I have a catalog of all the YWAM bases. I contacted the Grimerud base in Norway and they accepted Louise and me for two weeks in July. Norway? That's about as far-fetched as Hawaii. It was never on my radar, and now-

We flew to Oslo, and got a train to a station near the base. Someone from the base picked us up. The weather was great. Supper was outside in this beautiful pastoral landscape. The base is a large complex on a farm, buildings yellow or red. We were given very nice rooms and warmly welcomed.

Our job was to work in foods. We helped prepare the meals, serve, and the clean-up. The dining tables had to be wiped down and the floor swept and mopped.

Nina gave us our work assignments. We met Andreas and Heather, the base directors. There were 60 students doing a Mission Adventures training. They soon left to minister in Latvia, Lithuania, Romania, and Moldova. We did the housecleaning after they left.
That weekend we went on the "Norway in a Nutshell" tour, from Oslo to Bergen, by train. The scenery was lakes and mountains, plus we did a fjord boat trip, and a bus trip through the Stalheim Valley. In Bergen, we went to the waterfront. Bergen was a major European trading and seafaring port and one of the Hanseatic merchants' four most important trading centers. I was happy to see that row of picturesque houses.

On the return trip to Oslo, I got to do the Kon-tiki museum. I saw the Kon-tiki raft made of balsa wood, from the jungles of Peru.

The curator of the museum said one of the Peruvian men, who worked on the raft, once visited the museum and shared the trepidation most everyone felt about the voyage. I still say what a bunch of warriors! This was 1947. Some of these guys had just come out of the war with needed skills for this adventure and they were up to it. He pointed out the American flag that flew on the raft. Truman asked for the flag. It has been in the Truman library all this time. This year it is one hundred years since Heyerdahl's birth (1914-2014). They borrowed it to display for this centennial.

The next guests at the Y base were families doing a family camp. When they left, there was a debriefing conference for missionaries on the field to rest and recoup. We met interesting couples and heard their stories.

I had a lovely scene out my window I love to recall, also the fields of yellow wheat and red barns, good food and plenty of it. I especially remember fresh salmon. Oh, it was so good. Our friends were Nina, Neli, Esther, Sven Erik, Uddhav, Andreas and Heather. The beautiful Nordic people, blond-haired and blue-eyed. Especially the children. They remind me of porcelain dolls. I have wonderful memories of Norway. Someone took us to the station for the train to Oslo. We would fly to Prague in the Czech Republic.

In Prague, our hotel was near the Old Town Square and the astronomical clock. We did the walking tour. Callum was such a good guide I remembered a lot. He said France and England met with Hitler and sold Czechoslovakia out before the war. They told Hitler he could have the country if he would stop there. Of course he didn't. Callum told stories of resistance to the Nazi Movement. Two resistance fighters went after the "butcher of Prague" but things got fouled up and they were caught.

We passed the Jewish cemetery. They had to bury 12 bodies deep because they were not given more land. They lived in a ghetto and no matter how big the community got, the space of the ghetto stayed the same.

After the war, the Czechs were free of Hitler only to taken over by Communists. Finally, now, after independence, Czechoslovakia is divided into the Czech Republic and Slovakia.

There is a statue of Jan Hus in the square. He was a theologian. He preached in Prague in the 1300-1400's. Inspired by Wycliffe, he focused on radical reforms of the corrupt church. He was dangerous to the establishment and was burned at the stake. So the line-up is: Wycliffe, Hus, and then Luther, all of whom were reformers and precursors to the Protestant Reformation. This being 2017, it has been 500 years since Luther nailed his 95 theses on the church door at Wittenburg in 1517. I enjoyed learning about Hus and how he fits between Wycliffe and Luther.

We walked along the Charles Bridge and back to our favorite sidewalk restaurant for weiner schnitzel, potato salad, and Moravian cabbage. Actors in Don Giovanni passed by advertising the opera. We walked to the Vltava River and did a boat tour. The Bohemian city is so beautiful from the river. Louise and I had never been to Prague or to that part of the world. I just wanted to go there for years.

We flew to Venice to start our Italy trip. We got in at night and found the right vaporetto to take to our lodging. What an introduction to Venice- the Grand Canal at night. I was blown away. Louise had been to Italy before so she was a blessing in getting around. There is no way I could tell how it is be in Venice. There's no other place like that, the houses lining the water and the water slapping up onto steps with green algae and onto the board walks and sometimes right up to the doors. Many houses of beautiful architecture and grandeur. Lots of water traffic: gondolas, private boats, vaporettos, even cruise ships. In Venice there are roads for people to walk on, but no cars. All traffic is done on the canals. We mostly spent our time on the Grand Canal. It was relaxing to sit on the deck of the vaporetto and enjoy the view.

We took a train to Florence and a taxi to our convent. We took a bus to Santa Maria Nouvella and saw the altar where Galileo was denounced for his belief that the earth revolved around the sun. We saw the Medici chapels. The wealthy Medici family were patrons of artists Donatello, Botticelli, Leonardo, Raphael, and Michelangelo. We went to the Galleria Academia where Michelangelo's David is on display. We went in the Duomo, Florence's cathedral that literally dominates the skyline. Brunelleschi designed the huge dome. Sometimes we took a taxi. Sometimes we walked. The streets are narrow, lined with locals and tourists. The taxis and the buses and motorcycles just keep going very fast. They don't stop. The people just move over. It is crazy.

We went to Dante's house, author of <u>The Divine Comedy</u>. It may have been here we read about the florin. The Florentine gold coin was the standard coinage throughout Europe. The line at the Uffizi art gallery was too long. We skipped it. It holds works by da Vinci, Titian, Rembrandt and many artists.

We took a bus up a mountain, to Piazzale Michelangelo, and had a very good pizza, and took a photo of the city below with a nice shot of the Ponte Vecchio Bridge over the Arno River. Back to the city and did the Santa Croce church. Galileo and Michelangelo are buried there. So I guess we did the highlights of the city known for the birth of the Renaissance.

We took a train to Rome and a taxi to our convent in Trastavere, not so far from the Tiber. We did the Roman Forum. You think of the Senate, Caesar and Brutus. The ruins in the Forum are not significant or impressive. Time has erased so much of it. We walked to the Colosseum. It is hard to believe you are standing there with this iconic Roman ruin in front of you. I couldn't erase the images in my mind of the gladiators fighting to the death and Christians devoured by beasts for entertainment.

I thought the Victor Emmanuel monument was beautiful. He was the first king of united Italy. We did the Hop On-Hop Off bus, passed St Peters, the Colosseum, the Circus Maximus. We walked to the Trevi Fountain. It was in scaffolding.

We walked through St Peters. Bernini's column over Peter's tomb is pretty. He also designed the colonnade outside that frames in a semi-circle the courtyard of the Vatican. We saw Michelangelo's Pieta inside the Vatican and John Paul's tomb.

I did the Sistine Chapel. Louise had been. Louise went in the Basilica di San Giovanni founded by Constantine, once the papal residency. We sat on bleachers by Trajan's column and had an icecream. We went in Chiesa del Gesu where Ignatius Loyola who founded the Jesuits is buried. There was a beautiful musical rendering at his tomb. I wanted to see Italy leisurely, maybe live somewhere and connect with people. This trip was done as a tourist, but that has its rewards.

By the summer of 2015, Amy had sent me the Workaway website for those who want a volunteer experience. People in many countries post they need volunteers to work for room and board. Most of these people need physical labor. I found a summer camp in Ireland that needed English teachers. I paid the fee to Workaway and contacted John Grisewood who runs the summer camp. He could use me.

I flew into Shannon and took a bus to Limerick where John picked me up and took me to his farm in Ballyneety. It is a working farm with farm animals and gardens of vegetables, but he and Catherine who are retired school teachers have enjoyed working in summer camps for years, so he now has built accommodations to house campers and has contracts with people in Italy, Spain, Russia, to send a group of their kids to Ireland for camp to hone their English skills as well as have fun. I think he realized there was a market for camps with exposure to English and capitalized on it.

When the two groups arrived, one from Spain, one from Italy, we tested them for their efficiency level. We had four classes that rotated. Every teacher had an assistant and we chose our lessons from a group of prepared lessons or we improvised. Claire, from France, was my assistant and she was wonderful. The kids were middle school age and well-behaved and cooperative. I loved working with them.

Breakfast in the lunchroom. Classes in the morning. Then lunch. In the afternoons they did sports, go-carts, basketball, volleyball, horseback rides, trampoline, table tennis, billiard pool. Local Irish young people came out to the farm and hung out with the foreign kids, engaging them in conversation in English. Then we had one hour of homework. They had to write a short paper on an assigned topic. After supper, there were mystery tours. The kids were taken to a places such as to an old Norman tower not far from the farm or the Great Grange Stone Circle at Lough Gur.

The Vikings came to Ireland in the 700's, the Normans in the 1200's. The English started colonizing in the 1600's. Ireland fought for independence from England and finally won in 1921.

Some nights there would be Irish music in the dining room by local musicians. Or disco dancing. Or karaoke. There was always something for them to do. John is a ball of energy, so full of fun. The kids love him.

One night John took a group of us to a local pub. His brother, Paul, was playing the fiddle in the band.

On the week-ends John hires a bus and takes the kids, staff, and teachers to places accessible in a daytrip. While I was there, we went to Cobh, the last port of call for the Titanic. I enjoyed that. We went to the Cliffs of Moher, but the weather was horrific, rain and wind. You couldn't stand up to it. I went back to the bus. The kids went on but came back drenched. Another week-end we went to Galway. Aniko, a teacher from Hungary, and I hung out together. John ran the camp, but Seoirse, his brother-in-law, ran the school. He was so attentive to me and shared so much Irish history. I can tell you this. The Irish do not like the English. They had them in a choke hold for centuries. I have noted some things Seoirse shared. The Romans never went to Ireland, thus few large cities. The Romans built cities. Ireland never had resources to have industry, not part of the Industrial Revolution as in England. Small farms are the landscape and backbone of Ireland.

The English wanted to control the Irish. They confiscated land from the Irish and planted Protestant English and Scottish people in Northern Ireland, referred to as the Ulster Plantation. The Irish worked for a landlord, paid rent, and raised potatoes. At one time the Irish could not practice their Catholic faith or be educated. They were totally under English Protestant rule.

The famine was from 1845-1849. An airborne disease destroyed the potato crops. The people were starving and had no money. Many English landlords evicted the Irish families from their homes when they could not pay the rent. They were too weak to work in some public works projects. Millions died and millions immigrated. The famine was not totally caused by crop failure. It was genocide. The English shipped the food out of Ireland under guard to deliberately starve the people.

The Irish war of independence was fought from 1919-1921. They finally won independence after 800 years of subjugation by the English. Ireland was partitioned into the Irish Free State with Northern Ireland part of the UK.

Frank McCourt's bust at the Leamy School

Seoirse and Helen took Aniko and me to Limerick to Frank McCourt's museum which was a highlight of my trip. Frank wrote <u>Angela's Ashes</u>, a memoir of growing up in the lanes, dirt poor, starving; his brothers and a sister died. The father drank the wages when he did work. Frank's mother, Angela, and the four boys who lived had a hard life. Frank left for America at age 19, went to school, taught school 30 years and then wrote his memoir, receiving the Pulitzer Prize. I have followed him for years. He is no longer living. I was thrilled to do the museum which is housed in the Leamy School where the boys went as children.

There was an example of Frank's writing assignment when he went to school there. He wrote that it's a good thing Jesus wasn't born in Limerick. He would have died with consumption from the unrelenting rain and the cold weather. Frank was a hoot at age eleven.

Paul, John's brother, drove me to the airport which was wonderful and stayed with me up to security. That was a blessing. I tell you what. The experience of knowing John and being a part of life there was so unique. There is just no place like it anywhere. It was a once-in-a-lifetime experience. In the feedback on Workaway one volunteer said, "It's the craziest place on earth." Another said, "I left part of my heart there." I agree with both of them.

Venice and Cappadocia are unique because of place. The stone work in St Victor la Coste in France and the Ballyneety farm and school in Ireland are unique because of Gignoux and John.

Ukraine and Poland

2016

The workaway.info website is fun to peruse. I found a family in Ukraine who only wanted someone to converse with them in English. I found in Warsaw, Poland, a language immersion program needing teachers to work with Polish adults improving their English. These dates were two weeks apart. Then I found a YWAM base in Ukraine that would welcome us for one week in this interim. So the other week we could do the tourist thing. Louise and I were set for a five week adventure.

We flew to Kiev, Ukraine, where Roman and Katerina Kovalchuk met our plane and drove us to their house in Gostomel. We would stay with them for two weeks. The house is several stories with ivy covering the walls, yard beautifully landscaped. They have two daughters, Miroslava and Masha.

Roman and Katya posted their homestay on workaway, but did not expect any takers. This was around the time of the Ukrainian Revolution in 2014 and there was a lot of unrest. However, they have had many guests. They are forward-looking and determined to polish their English and broaden their world perspective. They love hosting people period, and they love the interchange of ideas and the chance to use and improve their English. They travel extensively and are just delightful to be with.

They took us to Kiev-Pechersk Lavra, a monastic abbey. We went down in the caves where the monks used to live. The Abbey is the Center of Eastern Orthodox Christianity in Eastern Europe and is a UNESCO World Heritage Site.

We went to St Sophia's Cathedral, and Andrew's Descent. They took us to Maidan Square where the protests to oust President Yanukovych took place from November 2013 to February 2014. After the break-up of the Soviet Union, Ukraine endured years of corruption and lack of economic growth. The country sought relationship with the EU. The president was to sign an agreement but then signed a treaty with Russia instead. Many people protested this in the Square and many were killed. The president fled to Russia. After that, Putin took the Crimea. (Khrushchev had given the Crimea to Ukraine.) There are speculations why he took it back. We later met Sharyn and Ruslan Borodin at the YWAM base who were living in Crimea at that time.

Roman said Russians have always had the mindset of power and conquering. They think of Ukraine as inferior to Russia. Roman loves Ukraine. It makes him mad to hear people speaking Russian! He said they should speak Ukrainian.

Maiden Square is on Khreschatyk Street. We walked Khreschatyk Street. It was Sunday. No cars on Sunday. Only pedestrians and people enjoying their leisure stroll. It is their most famous street flanked with buildings of beautiful architecture.

Roman was a parachutist in the Soviet Army before the regime fell. He was supposed to go to Siberia. His father helped get him stationed in Eastern Ukraine instead. When the Communist regime ended, Roman's father died. He was confused and upset when he lost his job, but, like Roman, he did not believe in the Communist system and the Soviet government.

Roman's grandfather was a high-ranking Communist. His grandmother liked church. She couldn't go because she had to protect him from church involvement, so women would come to her house to pray. He would just look the other way.

Katya cooked everyday wonderful Ukrainian dishes: borscht, dumplings, cabbage rolls, fried potato pancakes, carrot pancakes, squash, Russian potato salad, beets, carrots, eggplant, heavy on veggies. We picked cherries in the yard and made a cherry tarte.
We had a very lovely visit with Roman and Katya, many conversations on history, the Communist era, WWII, politics, travel. We said our good-byes as they put us on the train for Ternopil where we would volunteer at the YWAM base for one week.

YWAM staffers met our train. Lance and Megan Roberts are the directors of the base. A nice room was in readiness. Val and Yana are staff. We ate varenyky with them for supper. This is a staple Slavic fare, a small dough envelope filled with meat or veggie or fruit, pinched and boiled.

Our work assignment was to take many shelves of books down and classify them: biography, fiction, religion, history, etc: Louise also cut kitchen towels from a bolt of cloth to be hemmed later.

I was given a book from the library, The Little Town that Blessed the World. I love how this pulls together some pieces of early missions history for me. In Prague, I learned about Jan Hus whose followers were Hussites, persecuted by the established church. I read about Count Zinzendorf in Turkey. So, this book relates that in the early 1700's, Count Zinzendorf asked persecuted Hussites from Moravia to live on his property in Herrnhut along with other religious groups. They disagreed on doctrine. He was unable to establish unity until one night in a communion service, a powerful impartation of the Holy Spirit fell on them. Weeping, confession, and forgiveness flowed. Prayer meetings continued and resulted in establishing the Moravian Church and sending forth more missionaries than were sent in the past 200 years.

John Wesley had his personal encounter with salvation after meeting the Moravians. The Moravians' desire is to WIN FOR THE LAMB, THAT WAS SLAIN, THE REWARDS OF HIS SUFFERING. YWAM has a base in Herrnhut. I would love to go.

Louise and I went rambling. We got on the wrong bus going home and wound up at this old mill restaurant. Its authenic interior is decorated with antique items. So rustic and atmospheric. We had cucumber, tomato, red pepper, and sheep cheese salad, veal with onions in a cream sauce, and mashed potatoes.

A pretty waitress asked me how we found the meal. I thought she meant. "How did you find us?" I started telling how we got lost and just decided to get off the bus and there was the restaurant right before our eyes! She was listening politely. I finally realized she meant, "How did you like the meal?"

Rebecca and Roman Taturevych (yes, another Roman) from the base asked us over to eat. Delicious meal and berry pie and Roman does the dishes. Roman told about the Soviet rule. There was forced starvation in Ukraine under Stalin in 1932-33. Anyone who did not co-operate with the co-operative farming was sent to Siberia to die. If farmers kept their farms, they were in defiance. Seven million people perished in the breadbasket of Europe, with the people deprived of the food they had grown with their own hands. Roman told about a Russian holding forth the propaganda that the Russians believe. The man was telling how wonderful Russia was, everything was the best, Russia was the most wonderful place to live. A boy who did not make the connection, said, "Oh, I would love to live in that place." He did not realize the man was talking about where he lived because that is not the life he knew at all.

We enjoyed one of the prayer meetings at the base. The children of the staffers sang. We went to the English Club night and shared our stories. Finally, Lance and Megan took us to L'viv to catch our flight to Poland. Lance shared about YWAM. It is a heart school. Classes deal with your heart. You learn the Father's heart. You deal with your heart issues before you can minister to others.

I have to mention that we considered taking a train from Ukraine to Poland, but it seemed complicated. So we did a flight. Anyway, I wish I had done the train so I could tell this story. When you get to the border, the size of the tracks is different, so they have to lift the train and change the wheels. A Soviet thing. That would be a wild experience to tell.

We arrived in Krakow. I loved Krakow. We did a Chopin concert. A pretty lady and accomplished pianist. We did a museum of Polish history, a Jewish museum, a concert at St Peters and Pauls. A violinist was sitting outside the church playing beautiful music. We sat and listened. I can't express how I enjoyed that. We liked walking in the Market Square at night. Everything so lit up and many tourists. People just enjoying life. That particular night we had a lentil soup that was to die for.

We toured John Paul's house right across from Wawel Cathedral where he was archbishop before he was pope. That night we ate at the Morskie Oko Restaurant. We had pig knuckle, potato pancakes, cabbage, and icecream. Polish dancers came in and performed right by our table. A very beautiful restaurant and such a fitting ending to our last night in Krakow.

Train to Warsaw. Radio Café and stroganoff. The Uprising Museum. Here we learned that the Poles got enough of the Germans and tried to fight back in 1944. They thought the Russians would help them but they did not. Neither did the West. Churchill helped, but not the US. They were defeated and Warsaw was leveled. Our local paper featured a man who now lives in Jacksonville. He was part of the Polish Uprising at age 17.

We went to the Chopin monument, to the Marie Curie museum. We met the 'Just Speak' teachers for the Language Immersion Program at the Pizza Hut in Old Town Warsaw to get acquainted. The next day Malgosia picked us up at the hotel and we drove to a beautiful place in the country named Rancho Pod Bocianem which means Under the Storks Nest. Beautiful grounds. Huge blue spruces. We settled in our rooms. Supper was a meat, beets, and carrot slaw after a delicious hot soup. Every meal started with a very hot tasty soup.

This program has only been operating here maybe a year. Malgosia is an excellent director. We had eight teachers and four students, all Polish adults who want to improve their English skills. Andrew and Ivona are a doctor and dentist respectively. Adam in sales. Dorota, a math teacher. We had one-on-one sessions with them with prepared scripts to facilitate conversation. We played some fun games that pulled everyone into conversation and learning new words as well. The teachers were from Britain, the States, and Australia. We all got along and had fun in that environment. We had a diverse five weeks, a lot of variety, a good trip.

Very soon after I got home I had an ablation, the heart procedure they do to stop atrial fibrillation. Eventually, I got off the heart meds.

We had a tempestuous election year, all the way up to the night the returns came in. Many angry voters were tired of the elite establishment. Many voters were undecided, not happy with either candidate. Republican voters believe in a conservative ideology. We needed to vote for that platform regardless. Trump made extreme promises to repeal Obamacare, to close the border, address immigration, empower the blue collar worker again. We will see. Of major importance is appointing conservative Supreme Court judges to the bench. Many people feel that the dark cloud that has hung over us for eight years has been lifted.

Clinton was favored to win. Election night was a catastrophic surprise. We couldn't believe Trump went in. The media wants you to believe everyone in America is liberal but that is not true. I followed Franklin Graham's visit to every state capital. He held prayer rallies with big turnouts. I am glad that we had that many people who turned to God to intervene in a nation that is determined to turn from him.

The first weeks of his Presidency saw executive orders and a fast pace effort to fulfill his campaign promises. Many people were thrilled. Neil Gorsuch is confirmed for the Supreme Court. That is a good thing.

In my personal life, I enjoy services and fellowship with my Kingdom Life church family. Steve and Jackie Kuhn pastor several families. Tamar and Tucker Jackson, Debbie Freeman, Penny and Bob End, Marie and Bill Moore, Steven and Mary and Mark Kuhn. Pastor Steve is an excellent minister.

I have also begun playing handbells at Terry Parker Baptist Church, and joined their Keenager choir, and the Singing Seniors at Arlington Methodist Church.

Time for the Wycliffe banquet. Wycliffe Bible Associates puts on a banquet every year to raise awareness for Bible translation in countries where the people have no Bible in their heart language. Brent Nelson, the Area director, organizes these. Last year our speaker was Don Richardson, author of <u>Peace Child</u>. In 1962, Don and Carol went to live among the Sawi, headhunters and cannibals, in Irian Jaya Indonesia, in the western half of the island, New Guinea, with Papua New Guinea on the East. He designed an alphabet, taught them to read, translated the New Testament in their language. Carol's ministry was nursing. They were there 15 years.

The story is remarkable. Two tribes that were enemies decided to make peace. In their culture each tribe had to offer a child to the other tribe to raise. The men who gave their child – it had to be their only child. This act guaranteed the tribes would keep the peace. Don and Carol had made no inroads into the Sawi's understanding of the gospel to this point. So Don was ecstatic he could use this analogy to explain that God gave his only child to make peace between us and the True God forever. The Sawis understood and believed. Not only did they receive salvation, but the culture was revolutionalized as well as their ethics and value systems.

This year the speaker will be Grace Fabian. Her book is <u>Outrageous Grace</u>. She and her husband Edmund went to Papua New Guinea in 1969. Again he had to construct a written language. In 1993, after 24 years, he was nearly finished translating the New Testament into the Nabak language. Edmund and Grace were so happy they were nearly ready to complete a check list and publish the New Testament in Nabak.

A native who was working with him began hearing voices in his head. He could not get rid of them. They were driving him crazy. He picked up an ax to chop at the voices but instead chopped into Edmund's skull. Unbelievable agony for the family. Their son helped Grace finish the New Testament translation.

There are many people groups in the world that do not have the scripture in their language. Missionaries with Wycliffe Bible Translators have started 2,771 New Testament translations while 3,771 are not started. It is a big task but so worth it when people have scripture in their heart language. Advances in high tech computer equipment have enabled translators to accomplish their work much faster.

I decided to try my hand at blogging recently, book critiques and short travelogues, featuring some really nice photos of the travels described in this book. I couldn't put the pictures in this book. Please enjoy them in the blogs.

The link is
musingsofmarilyn.wordpress.com/blog/

Then friends encouraged me to write my book. My friend Frances said, "Marilyn, just write it. You are running out of time." As I lived through all of this again, it seems like God has been chasing me down to bless me, a lot of hard places but some of the journey a pleasure of serendipitous turns.

I have a desire to press into God. Many testimonies inspire me. Randy Clark's story and Leif Hetland's are a testimony to God's grace. Francis and Judith MacNutt have a worldwide Christian

Healing Ministry based here in Jacksonville. They teach salvation, healing, and deliverance.

They teach that if you do not grow up feeling loved and comfortable with who you are, a false self develops out of the need for survival. That self attaches itself to various addictions and is looking for love. Many times hurtful things in the past help to destroy this already needy person. The MacNutts have found that they can pray for people, and the Holy Spirit can meet them, as they remember those hurtful memories when they were a child. The Holy Spirit can love on that person, free them from the bondage of the memory, and cause them to find their true self. They are set free from the crippling memory to live a normal, wholesome life. This powerful method of prayer is called inner healing.

Reinhard Bonnke is also an inspiration. He has an interesting story full of miracles, told in <u>Living a Life of Fire</u>. In WWII, the family lived in East Prussia. His father, Hermann, fought for Germany. When things came down in 1945, and the Russians were moving in to finish off Germany, Reinhard was four. His father had to stay with the troops. His mother and four siblings made a hair-raising run under strafing fire to a ship and to Denmark, but not to safety. They were soon in a prison camp there for years. Hermann was in a British prisoner-of-war camp in in West Germany.

In the camp, Hermann was praying. A man in white in middle Eastern sandals, long hair and a full beard, approached him, smiling. It was Jesus. Dan Baumann, whom I met at the YWAM base in Jacksonville, was also visited by Jesus in Evin Prison in Iran. I cannot imagine what that encounter meant to them.

The Bonnke family was reunited in 1949. Hermann Bonnke pastored a Pentecostal church in Gluckstadt. Reinhard was tapped by God at age ten to bring the gospel to Africa. Over the years, seventy-three million have come to Christ and thousands have been healed.

Most of the church world knows of Heidi and Rolland Baker's story of miracles, told in their book, <u>Always Enough.</u> Such a testament to God's heart of love. They have helped many hundreds of throw-away children in Mozambique, one of the poorest places on earth. The children, ravaged by civil war, poverty, rape and trauma, are carried up in visions to heaven. They meet and talk with Jesus. They are loved on, healed, and many become pastors. Five thousand churches have been planted.

I love how God has invaded these people after God's heart and is using them in many salvations and healings, with them only a conduit. I think ministries like these showcase what Jesus said. When Jesus came, he said, "The kingdom of heaven is at hand." In other words, "I have come and I have brought my world with me."

Bill Johnson quotes, "The testimony of Jesus is the spirit of prophecy." Meaning, telling others what Jesus has done in your life can "foretell" faith to explode in those who hear your testimony. People begin to expect and see miracles in their own lives because the stories you tell them reveal who God really is. I believe the testimonies in this book will increase faith. I want heaven to invade earth for us who desire it and who keep on keeping on even when we get side-tracked.

> "Prone to wander, Lord I feel it.
> Prone to leave the God I love.
> Praise the mount. I'm fixed upon it.
> Mount of thy redeeming love."

"Thy kingdom come. Thy will be done. On <u>earth</u> as it is in <u>Heaven</u>."